Zona Home

Zona Home

ESSENTIAL DESIGNS FOR LIVING

Louis Sagar

DESIGNED BY
GREG SIMPSON & ERIC BAKER
ERIC BAKER DESIGN ASSOCIATES

TEXT WRITTEN
WITH LISA LIGHT

MANAGING EDITOR
MARTI SAGAR

HarperStyle

An Imprint of HarperCollinsPublishers

HarperCollins books may be purchased for educational,

business, or sales promotional use.

For information please write:

Special Markets Department,

HarperCollins Publishers, Inc.,

10 East 53rd Street,

New York, NY 10022.

FIRST EDITION

Library of Congress Cataloging-in-Publication Data

Sagar, Louis.

Zona home : essential designs for living / by Louis Sagar. — 1st ed.

p.   cm.

ISBN 0-06-270169-X

1. Interior decoration. 2. House furnishings. 3. Decoration and ornament. I. Title.

TX311.S25   1995

640—dc20   96-6195

96 97 98 99 00 ❖/P 10 9 8 7 6 5 4 3 2 1

T*his*
book is dedicated to my mom,
Beatricia Sagar,
who gave me my creative spirit,
and to my dad,
Skip Sagar, who gave me the
drive and vision.

Contents

Introduction

I n 1980, the year I opened Zona in SoHo, the popularity of modernist home design was at its peak. The look was cool, clean, and very urban. Home furnishings were highlighted by polished chrome, black lacquer, and beveled glass. Anything natural felt unnatural. Just pick up an interior home magazine from the late 1970s and you'll see what I mean. I would look at spreads from those magazines and find little inspiration in their exalted homages to modernity.

At this time, I was absorbing a growing environmental consciousness. The health of the planet was endangered, so much so that a safe future seemed to require a fundamental shift in thinking. I was energized by the strong realization that the global village was indeed a reality. The planet was feeling smaller; resources were finite. I recognized that one could no longer do something in one part of the world without having an impact in another, often distant part. At Zona I understood and tried to articulate those essential links between your home, my home, and the larger habitat of the Earth by focusing on the hand-made and natural materials. I wanted to establish a bridge between the artisan, who offered access to those materials by fashioning them into useful forms, and the growing number of people who had interest in restoring a natural sensibility to their homes. This dedication to the universal influence of artisans and craft is at the heart of my design ethic. It symbolizes the best fusion of the hand and the material, and provides our homes with a strong sense of integrity.

I didn't have a grand plan to revive the natural in the home when I started Zona. My design philosophy was simply an extension of a childhood that encouraged a theatrical way of thinking and rewarded creative exploration. I was just working on how to keep myself inspired and how to ask the right questions. As a logical step in that journey, Zona was founded to serve as a space in which to sustain an evolving aesthetic.

The Zona concept was, and is, about asking questions, sharing information, and presenting an ever-changing assortment of products and services. The objects I've collected are symbolic of the

"AT A TIME WHEN THE EVER-EXPANDING PRESENCE OF ELECTRONIC TOOLS AND HIGH TECHNOLOGY IS SO PERVASIVE, THE NEED TO BALANCE OUR LIVES WITH PRODUCTS THAT CELEBRATE THE TEXTURAL AND SENSORIAL BECOMES ESSENTIAL. ZONA REFLECTS A STRONG COMMITMENT TO QUALITY, INTEGRITY IN DESIGN, BEAUTY, AND A SENSE OF VALUE FOR THE HOME. WE ARE GUIDED BY THE BELIEF THAT INFORMATION IS ENERGY AND CHANGE IS CONSTANT."—ZONA MISSION STATEMENT, CIRCA 1980

search, and are to be absorbed as much through the simple pleasure of observation as through acquisition. Each day I explain to people how Zona is built upon that feeling of exploration and discovery. First-time visitors will often comment, "Well, what is It?" My answer is, usually, that's exactly it.

Every aspect of Zona, from the thematic influences in visual presentation to the selection of individual items, is a direct result of questions, not answers. It's amazing to me that many people come to Zona to experience the environment alone, to indulge their curiosity by tuning in to the sounds, the smells, or the placements of objects in the space. People visit Zona from around the world and take time to pause as if they were walking in the park. They respond to the atmosphere and to the daily changes of the space. They experience a real sense of comfort and warmth.

Zona is still evolving. Even today, a note pad for jotting down brainstorms and a flash of visual inspiration are my best design tools. My great creative passion has always been, simply, to set up situations in which people are surprised by the unexpected, and to produce environments that are stimulating to the senses. These dynamics are never engendered in direct response to a prevailing trend; rather, they are an ongoing expression of one's travels and experiences. I can think of no better place to cultivate and honor that sense of personal experience than one's own home.

I have always thought of Zona as a laboratory for discovering the ways in which we can make our homes comfortable. Our increasingly complex society compels us, now more than ever, to turn to our homes as the primary energy centers in which to nurture ourselves by celebrating the textural and sensorial.

This is my cookbook. Let me know what you think of the recipes.

1

Feeling at Home

What Is

"Make yourself at home" is a remark we often make to people when they arrive at our house. This easy phrase infers a collective intimacy, an extension of welcome that opens up onto the informal and comforting flow of life in our household. We all want to share that sense of comfort we have in our homes with our family and friends. And it's ultimately the creation of such comfort that's important to us when we begin to live on our own. As we settle down, the comfort of home resides in a growing sense of self-determination: in decor, in location, and mostly in the knowledge that only we can find what it is that we are looking for there. ¶ When we acknowledge the importance of home, we are taking note of ourselves. Home is ultimately the place in our lives that is uniquely ours, a flexible space reflecting where we come from and how we got here. The home becomes the canvas on which we express our own viewpoint and sense of style. Once we arrive at that place, however, we often become overwhelmed with how much there is to do. We have the desire to make the effort, but we are unsure how to start or where to begin. We can change this feeling by adjusting our point of view so that we can enjoy the process of creating home, over time. ¶ It is important to respect the fact that we can never do everything we want in our homes all at once. When we are starting out, for example, we may have the time, but *we might not have the necessary resources. Later on, we may have the experience and the means, we know our routines and what we need from our space, but we often do not have sufficient quality time to make changes. To counter the sometimes overpowering scope of the vision we want to achieve, it is helpful to break down home-making activities into small steps with simple goals. In this way you can keep expectations in balance with a realistic estimation of available time. Almost any project can be broken down into phases. ¶ When embarking on creating a home, remember always to make yourself at home first. Rather than having your home-making agenda force an impractical lifestyle on your household, ensure that all tasks feel achievable: work them into your daily routine, and strive for consistency in your effort. With larger projects, like painting and renovating, work at making the completion of each phase feel rewarding. Whatever we do, we need to work harder at setting ourselves up for success. Pride of place has a great deal to do with pride of accomplishment.*

Home?

The Mission of Home

I think we all have original thoughts on what "home" means in our own lives. We know that homes are made up of rooms to serve our specific needs for living, but have we determined for ourselves how home serves us emotionally? The Zona home first defines a space by answering this question. Designing a mission statement for the home helps establish priorities and provides invaluable guidelines for the unique sense of place we are seeking to create.

HOME IS A SHELTER, a safe space with physical boundaries designed to meet the daily demands of cover and comfort we must provide for ourselves and our families.

HOME IS A SHRINE, in which to celebrate a natural, textural, and elemental relationship to nature.

HOME IS A THEATER, a place to express our imagination, cultivate taste, and develop an aesthetic identity that builds inner strength and self-confidence.

HOME IS AN ARCHIVE, in which we memorialize key experiences, tell the stories of our lives, and document formative moments in the history of our family.

HOME IS A SANCTUARY, for the nurturing of one's soul, where we absorb and reflect on the world around

us and pay homage to our legacy of family wisdom.

HOME IS A TERRITORY, in which we stake our claim to personal space.

The creation of a mission statement for your home is a personal testament of your goals. Allow that statement to change over time as your needs and aspirations grow. For example, the mission statement I recently wrote is much more concrete than the one I developed for both my home and for Zona fifteen years ago:

Today, I want a home that provides safety and comfort for my family without compromising on space for creative expression. I want to share my enjoyment in meeting artisans from around the world by collecting their crafts and presenting them meaningfully in my space. I want my home to feel caring and cared for, and gentle and congruous with my deep respect for Planet Earth.

In 1980, I focused the service of my space on a philosophy and emphasized "a presentation of product that seeks to balance technology with a celebration of the natural, textural, and sensorial." I have remained faithful to that philosophy over the years, yet I have learned, primarily through practice, how to execute my mission in more and more specific ways. One of the important insights of the Zona home is that as your goals become more refined and particular over time, you will gain the confidence to achieve them according to your own tastes and style, and your space will reward you with greater intimacy and comfort.

Writing a mission statement once a year helps to reacquaint you with your priorities and to record the changes you've made in your philosophies and home-making routines. Try keeping all the statements in a notebook or folder as a document of the evolving face of your own home.

A CONTEMPLATIVE VIEW OF THE MOUNTAINS OF FRANCONIA, MAINE.

Welcome Yourself Home

A SENSE OF PLACE

We cannot begin to create a home if we are not there ourselves. When we leave our first home to attend school or learn a trade, we begin what will be a formative cycle of living, often for short periods of time, in different spaces and environments. We move easily today. We live in dorms, put packs on our backs. We are busy tending to our careers and building personal relationships. We travel around trying to find the right place in which to settle down. And we move through lots of rooms along the way.

We start out living in small apartments in cities and towns. We buy our first bed or our first sofa. Eventually we get rid of the hand-me-downs and the used pieces and invest in our own furnishings. Tight budgets make our approach to creating home feel compromised and con-strained. The available choices may disappoint us or pro-voke indecision; yet, we continue the cycle of acquisition—gather possessions, accumulate stuff. At some point, we begin to feel a deeper yearning for settlement. We all at once want a place of our own, a place to anchor all our belongings, a place to call home. The truth is, we begin building our home long before we arrive there.

Whether you are always on the move, living in tempo-rary quarters, or preparing to settle into a more permanent place, it can prove very helpful to begin noting ideas and inspirations for your home. Build a reference guide and identify your own special needs. The process alone will provide an excellent frame of reference, a workout for developing your sense of place, which will become an extension of yourself.

A Checklist to Plan for Your Ideal Home

This exercise will help you determine your own idea of home, independent of necessity, budget, or current fashion. Your sensibility evolves as your resources and needs change, so refer to and update this workbook whenever you need a touchstone to reaffirm your viewpoint and your own sense of style.

TAKE A VISIT TO YOUR LOCAL ARTS AND CRAFTS SUPPLY STORE and buy a sketchbook or several large roomy files and file boxes. Label each file or section with a category: for example, rooms, interior styles, or architectural details. Make your system as functional as possible for cataloging impromptu flashes and sketches, and for storing photos, cut-out ideas from fashion and home magazines, and sample swatches. Staying organized will be

simple and fun, and will afford you easy reference in the future.

VISUALIZE FIRST WHERE YOUR IDEAL HOME IS LOCATED: Is it on an island, an avenue, a street, a lane, or an alley? Place your home in a geographical setting: Is it in the countryside, near the beach, by the mountains, in the desert, in the city? Gather up pictures from magazines, or your own travels, to establish this sense of place.

THINK ABOUT WHAT SORT OF ARCHITECTURAL SPACE YOU WANT TO LIVE IN. Your home could be a loft or a cottage; it could be a log cabin, a brownstone, or even an empty lot.

WRITE AN IMAGINARY DESCRIPTION OF THE SPACE AND ITS SURROUNDING ENVIRONMENT. Make note of details like the structure's age, the materials from which it's built, and the types of plants and trees on the property.

MAKE UP AN ADDRESS FOR YOUR HOME. Write it on a label and attach it to the front of your portfolio, to formalize and validate your homework.

THINK ABOUT COLOR—THE COLORS YOU LIKE TO LIVE WITH. Gather up sample paint chips, or fragments of natural elements that evoke the palette you'd like to create. Write descriptions of these colors, and be specific. It's fun to make up names for them, so give it a try. Collect postcards of your favorite paintings to create a reference file for color.

IMAGINE THE PASSAGEWAYS AND FLOW OF ACTIVITY THROUGH ALL THE ROOMS OF YOUR HOME. Think of your

PREPARE AN INVENTORY OF ESSENTIALS FOR EACH ROOM IN YOUR HOME: things that go beyond the basics (i.e., towels and dishes), but are conceived of as fundamental to your sense of comfort, more than simple amenities. Be as detailed as you can. If you love to cook, for example, then emphasize this aspect of your lifestyle. Never hesitate to change or update your "essentials" listing. It will remain a very important reference guide if it's kept current.

DESCRIBE THE ROOM OR PLACE THAT IS MOST FUNDAMENTAL TO YOUR FEELING OF HOME. Take time to think

home as if you were making a map: one part outlining the functional needs and necessities, the other part focused on the decorative and artistic.

DECIDE ON THE MOST IMPORTANT FURNISHINGS YOU WOULD BRING WITH YOU TO A NEW SPACE. Identify your true heirlooms. Write a story card on each heirloom, and create a record of all the furnishings and objects that have become an integral part of your home life.

about and designate the spaces for privacy and community you will need to establish in order to feel at home.

MAKE A LIST OF ALL THE THINGS YOU LIKE TO COLLECT. Try to describe how you might display the collections as groupings in your home. Then make a list of the things you have collected that you would prefer to throw away but to which you remain attached. Give some thought to how you might simplify unwanted collections and start implementing changes immediately. If you cannot eliminate all at once, try taking small steps, but be consistent.

MOVEMENT AND CHANGE HELP US ADDRESS WHICH BELONGINGS AND ROUTINES ARE FUNDAMENTAL TO OUR SENSE OF HOME. Practice expressing the comfort and feeling of home wherever you are, for however long you are there. When you finally arrive at the place in which you can truly settle, your notebooks and files will be brimming with ideas and inspirations.

Crossing the Threshold

SAFE PASSAGE

The map of your home begins at its threshold. Doors and openings are the main thoroughfare, connecting the world outside to your sanctuary within. Hallways and foyers will set the stage for the style in which the rest of your home unfolds. So, before you engage in the serious effort of comprehensive interior design, it is essential to give special consideration to the important entryways of your home. The threshold of your front door

scarves, and to store shoes. Save a spot for keys. Evaluate the flexibility of this reception area. When you come inside, is there an accessible place nearby, like a console table, to set down the mail and other packages, and that you can dress up when you have guests over?

Mirrors hung just inside of an entryway create a good flow of energy. Lighting should never be too bright in an entry; it should be warm and low, acting as a mediator

COLLECTIONS OF MEANINGFUL OBJECTS, WHETHER UTILITARIAN OR MERELY DECORATIVE, ADD CHARACTER AND COMPOSITIONAL STRENGTH TO AN ENTRYWAY. NATURAL LIGHT MOVING INSIDE FROM OUTDOORS CONTRIBUTES TO A SENSE OF INTIMACY AND WELCOME IN THIS IMPORTANT SETTING.

provides an excellent starting point for the practice of balancing function and comfort.

Start the process from the outside. Paint your front door a special color and place a small textural wreath or seasonal element on it. Hang a special placard of numbers identifying your address, and be creative—stay away from the generic numbers you'll find in the hardware store. Moving inside, take care to place a welcome mat just after the entry. Do your best to have a place to hang coats, umbrellas, hats and

between the diffused natural light of the outdoors and more vivid composed light within. A textural or floral element of some kind should greet you when you walk inside. The acoustics of this space should be low and hushed, to allow for adaptation between outdoor and indoor sounds. Keep these atmospheric elements fresh and uncluttered. Allow them to fill the space through suggestion. Communicating an aura of openness will result in safe passage for the spirit of warmth and welcome throughout the rest of your home.

Setting Up a Home

Crossing the threshold gives us an initial focal point for our sense of home. Let's take a look at a few additional steps to employ when we are preparing to move into a new place, or revitalizing a place we have been living in for a while.

1. GET FAMILIAR WITH THE SPACE. Always try to explore the rooms while they are empty. Make note of the entryways and exits. Where are the windows? Where become attuned to aspects of the space you did not notice before.

3. KNOW YOUR NEEDS. The basic dedications of space for cooking, eating, sleeping, washing, relaxing, and working should be clear. Evaluate whether the assignment of space to fit your family's needs is defined well enough.

4. GIVE CAREFUL THOUGHT TO YOUR OWN SPECIFIC ROUTINES AND FUNCTIONAL REQUIREMENTS. Envision yourself

are the stairways? Observe the proportions of the rooms, their width and height and depth. Examine the structural materials and the condition of the floors. Make note of any unusual architectural details, often hidden beneath layers of paint. Try and get a feel for the flow of natural light, and observe the resulting exposures of each room.

2. BEFRIEND THE SPACE. If you can, place a small chair in the center of the room and sit down. Take a look around for a few quiet minutes. Try it again from the corners. You will going through a typical workday and a typical weekend day. Pay attention to larger rooms, which can, and may need to, serve more than one function.

5. ADEQUATE STORAGE IS A KEY TO BEING ORGANIZED. The best of us have more than we can easily handle. A comprehensive inventory, and system, of storage for your belongings deserves high priority in your home-making plans. We all end up needing more storage than we think; advance planning and designating storage space for important items will help you make the most of the available storage.

6. CLASSIFY YOUR POSSESSIONS AS SACRED, ESSENTIAL, FUNCTIONALLY NECESSARY, AND NONESSENTIAL. In packing and storing, use thick black markers to label boxes according to their contents. Use every spring cleaning and moving opportunity to evaluate whether you need to hold on to articles that are nonessential—this will reduce the pressure to find new storage for them. Be objective about possessions that are no longer important to you. Give away whatever cannot be easily sold to someone who might appreciate it. Donate or recycle the rest. If you are moving from one home to another, pack anything truly sacred last and unpack it first.

the potential for unwanted noise. Ask a friend to go into an adjoining room and speak to him—how far does the sound carry? The acoustics of the space and the circulation of sound are very important to make note of so that you can dedicate quieter activities to quieter rooms.

9. HAVE AN EXTRA SET OF KEYS MADE. Honor a trusted friend with your keys and a nice bottle of wine. Make this action a gesture of thanks and a bond of faithful welcome to your home.

10. CREATE A SPACE FOR RETREAT OR A SPOT FOR A SHRINE. Place some of your important objects, heirlooms, and precious valuables within this space. Always let the

7. PURIFY AND CLEAN THE SPACE. First, open the windows. Let the fresh air circulate. Use incense or traditional sage smudge sticks to perform the ancient ritual of burning out disruptive spirits, and expel the stale scents in your space. Use a plant mister and create a citrus spray with fresh lemon, lime, or grapefruit juice mixed with water and a few drops of almond oil. Mist each room after you clean. The citrus will balance well with the smoky aroma of dried herbs or incense.

8. LISTEN TO THE SOUNDS OF THE SPACE. Different sounds emerge at different times of day, so be attentive to

kids participate in setting up their rooms and setting out their own special things. Encourage their creative interaction with the home at large, as well. In a new space, engage yourself with a sense of responsibility and look forward to the process of making it feel like a home.

11. DEFINE WHERE YOU WILL NEED OUTSIDE HELP OR SERVICE. Whether you consult a friend or a professional, a clear definition of your needs will enable design and space planning solutions to be determined effectively and economically.

Homesteading

"HOMESTEADING, AS I ENVISION IT,
IS OUR PROCESS OF REDEFINING THE PURPOSE OF THE
HOME TO FIT A NEW SET OF LIFESTYLE VALUES. I THINK
OF HOMESTEADING TODAY AS AN
ATTITUDE OF MIND THAT RECOGNIZES THAT THERE ARE
FEW NATURAL PLACES REMAINING IN THE WORLD FOR
PIONEERS TO SETTLE."

—LOUIS SAGAR

Making a "homestead," for most of the nineteenth and early twentieth century, was a consequence of pioneering the land. Government offers prompted enterprising citizens to move West and forced settlement of the new frontier. Pioneers dedicated themselves to the taming of a vast wilderness and the expansion of their country, and were rewarded with ownership of the land they cultivated. These homesteaders saw the opportunity to work hard, earn property, and establish a life based on a spirit of community. I am reclaiming the term "homesteading" and updating its meaning for now, because I believe it symbolizes the spirit of settlement needed to carry the idea of home into the next century.

Homesteading, as I envision it, is our process of

THE ORIGINAL HOMESTEADERS MOVED WEST, PIONEERING THE LAND WITH FAITH FOR A BETTER LIFE.

redefining the purpose of the home to fit a new set of lifestyle values. I think of homesteading today as an attitude of mind that recognizes that there are few natural places remaining in the world for pioneers to settle. The pioneering to be done now is in how to add meaning to the pursuit of livelihood, how to bring family and work back into balance, and how to embrace technology so that it soothes and aids, and does not alienate, us. The frontier is right here, within our homes, still defining our sense of place.

For example, in recent years many people have proclaimed the need to "get away" to someplace else in order to feel a connection to the land. A cabin in the mountains, a cottage on a lake, or a country home out of town—all have become important places of refuge. The traditional summer home is now a weekend getaway, to be used whenever the kids are out of school and on all the holidays. The family gathers here, and the time spent together is of a much higher quality than what is experienced back "at home." We are using the second home to pioneer better relationships to both nature and family. We have come to realize that these connections are an essential part of living, in the greatest sense, and we have rediscovered that old spirit of community. I like to think we are all becoming pioneers again, in that we are asking questions about the way of the future and doing what we can to bring our lives into balance and our homes into harmony with the environments we do live in.

OPPOSITE: "A RUSTIC ONE-ROOM CABIN, DESIGNED BY ABIGAL SHACHAT, STAKES A CLAIM FOR URBAN TRANSFORMATION, AN IDYLLIC RETREAT FOR DREAMING UP NEW IDEAS."

SoHo, New York

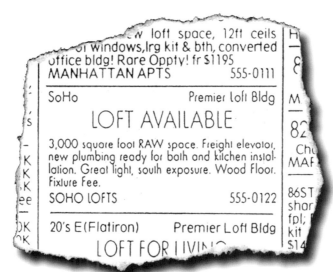

In a sense, the pioneering spirit is as alive today as it was a hundred years ago. Just visit SoHo, a reclaimed industrial district in lower Manhattan, to witness firsthand the results of modern homesteading.

In the late 1970s, SoHo was an abandoned territory with no parks and no trees. Nothing at all made the area feel like home. It was structurally gray and desolate. As is often the case, it took a migration of artists, desperate for space, to discover the foundations of a neighborhood. They saw that the big empty buildings with high ceilings and wonderful light could be reclaimed and revitalized into what we know today as loft living. In 1980, when I opened Zona in SoHo, artists were running around making deals with landlords for entire floors and abandoned buildings. Claims were being staked. The experience of owning "raw" space was exciting and captivating. I was attracted by the energy and creative spirit artists brought to the area. At Zona I perceived this new lifestyle ethic poking through all the brick. You could feel it growing before it actually flowered at the surface. Certainly, SoHo was becoming a neighborhood for a community of creative and artistic people who had grown tired of impermanence and wanted a place to both live and work.

Although I did not realize it at the time, Zona was destined to be the ideal SoHo store. I was surrounded by a totally new kind of aesthetic environment that was in perfect synch with my ideas about home not fitting into the shape of a house. In SoHo, the city had revealed a new frontier, and we homesteaders took to nurturing it like the most sacred plot of land.

SIMPLIFY YOUR LIFE

Elaine St. James's little book *Simplify Your Life: Ways to Slow Down and Enjoy the Things That Really Matter* has been a Zona bestseller. Elaine's most recent effort, *Inner Simplicity*, continues the quest. By contrast, ten years ago, the bestselling book at Zona was *Santa Fe Style*, by Diane Mather, which was a terrific book that identified the then-little-known Southwest interior style for people across the country. We were indeed interested in the outer skin ten years ago. Today, however, many of us seem focused on the inner skin. The pioneering work we must do, and an essential aspect of the Zona home, is to make our homes the central forum for addressing the quest toward inner harmony. This contemplative search will enrich the surface beauty of our world as we become more involved in what serves than in what merely decorates.

THIS STILL LIFE WITH SCULPTURAL LIVING PLANTS AND AN ELEGANT LANDSCAPE PAINTING OFFERS A WINDOWLIKE
VIEW WITHIN THE HOME ONTO THE WORLD OF NATURE.

Bring the Garden Indoors

HOME IS A TOTAL HABITAT

You don't need to create a second home in order to restore the balance of nature in your life; you needn't even live rurally. At Zona, as we found ourselves working and living in the city, with few parks and limited access to the countryside, we learned early to bring the garden inside. No matter where we live, the lesson has proved to be a rich one: The simple experience of potting a plant or bringing a fountain indoors does more than give us a healing dose of nature; it helps us bring down the barriers that bar outdoor elements from the traditionally conceived shelter of home. Home becomes a total habitat. And, with natural materials—water, stones, branches, plants, flowers—we gain access to a whole new world of sensory inspiration. The colors, textures, and sounds of nature enrich and pacify our space. We slow down. We are touched.

Early in Zona's history, I made a memorable pilgrimage to Palo Alto, California, to visit Paul Hawken and David Smith, founders of the garden supply catalog Smith and Hawken. At the time, they had just recently begun selling fine English gardening tools through the mail. They didn't have any plans to sell the tools to wholesalers; however, my persistence and sincer-

ity somehow prevailed, and Paul allowed me to display and sell the collection in my shop.

Of course, there was no grass at Zona, and certainly not a garden in sight in SoHo, but I was thrilled to be bringing symbols of the outdoors into the context of the city home. I was convinced that the tools would help me demonstrate that getting back to the land was important and bringing nature into the home vital.

BRINGING FAVORITE COLLECTIBLES OUT TO THE GARDEN EXTENDS THE LIVING SPACE OF YOUR HOME.

Paperwhites

I t has been more than twelve years since we first began selling wonderfully fragrant paperwhite narcissus bulbs at Zona. Here was a flowering plant that would simply grow and grow and grow, indoors, without much attention. The aroma of the narcissus is so penetrating that people often sit and tell stories of how this tiny flower had miraculously perfumed their homes when they come to Zona for more bulbs.

My effort at Zona to encourage people to plant a bulb, cultivate it, and enjoy its growth was an extremely important gesture during the early days. When we first introduced the concept of bringing the garden indoors, selling the beautiful Smith and Hawken garden tools and outdoor furniture, we were branching out into uncharted territory. We wanted to shift people's perception of what an urban home could accommodate. And we wanted to show that the dreary, gray months of cold in our winter climate could be countered indoors with greenery and flowering plants. Bringing the garden inside, season by season, has now become a tradition.

Paperwhites and other indoor bulbs can easily be grown between October 1 and the end of April. Planted bulbs will usually take four to six weeks to bloom. Other varieties to try include amaryllis and tulips, which will provide amazing bursts of color without any fragrance. Here is our recipe for growing paperwhites:

Select a decorative planter or bowl and fill it two-thirds full with pebbles and stones. Place the paperwhite bulbs on top of the pebbles. Add water up to the base of the bulbs. Gently place any extra pebbles around the bulbs to hold them in place and to fill the bowl. Place the bowl of paperwhites in bright, indirect sunlight. Avoid placing the bowl near any direct heat source. Add water as needed and watch them grow.

THE PAPERWHITE'S DELICATE PROFUSION OF FLOWERS AND LONG GREEN LINES LOOK BEST WHEN PRESENTED IN CLEAN, VERTICAL REPETITION.

Home in Balance

Today I sometimes think that we city dwellers take the natural less for granted than the suburban or rural dweller, simply because we have so much less access to real nature. Consequently, at Zona I try to teach people not to take any home environment for granted, for nature may be closer than you think. Nature can be a high-rise view of the park or a pot of grass growing on a fire escape as much as it can be a backyard or a dirt road bordered by day lilies and clover. This lesson comes out of respect for the uniqueness of each different sort of habitat people live in. Ultimately, any home is made up of diverse components, merged at will and without regard to what came locally and what came from afar. The cultural is mixed in with the natural; work life is mixed in with domestic life; friends are mixed in with family; neighborhood is mixed in with the global community. The integration of all these disparate elements creates the dynamic web of a home in balance. The tools for dialogue are at hand; our stories are waiting to unfold.

Our experience in helping people create total homes by tuning their senses was inspired by the desire to achieve a "high touch" environment. For example, when you are outdoors you can't help but take in the fragrance and color and shapes that surround you; when you are in a museum, your senses are moved by many of the same elements. Keeping home in balance with nature is a special calling, and means that we must be responsible enough to practice outside what we practice inside. Thinking of the planet at large as "home" is the way to conserve it for future generations, and the more we bring natural materials into the home, the more we learn to respect their source, our planet. When we bring a cord of firewood inside for our fireplaces, we remember the forest. We remember the orchards and fields and local farmers as we gather fruits and fresh vegetables for our table. Naturalness is as much a mandate for the home as comfort. If we are gentle in our honoring of the Earth, we will also learn to be gentle with the people and possessions in our physical community of home. A home in balance is our most valued heirloom.

"PEOPLE CANNOT LIVE APART FROM NATURE; AND YET, PEOPLE CANNOT LIVE IN NATURE WITHOUT CHANGING IT. WHAT WE CALL NATURE IS, IN A SENSE, THE SUM OF THE CHANGES MADE BY ALL THE VARIOUS CREATURES AND NATURAL FORCES IN THEIR INTRICATE ACTIONS AND INFLUENCES UPON EACH OTHER AND UPON THEIR PLACES. THE MAKING OF THESE DIFFERENCES IS THE MAKING OF THE WORLD. . . . NATURE, THEN, IS NOT ONLY OUR SOURCE BUT ALSO OUR LIMIT AND MEASURE."

—WENDELL BERRY

In the Element of Earth

Autumn

Earth. Soil and sand and water massaged into the form of clay. Harvested from the earth like so many other crops, clay goes back to the beginning of civilization and working it remains the lifeblood of utilitarian craft today. Pottery, the most universal of all crafts, has been produced by almost every culture, past and present. It is simply molded and baked earth—terra cotta.

FOR THE ARTISAN, ARTISAN LIFE IS LIFE ITSELF.

Italy

Italy is of the earth. The food, the wine, the soft, richly colored fabrics all speak from the soil. The grounded heart of Italy remains in the countryside—small villages and ancient towns are so organic in form and color, they appear as if they were carved out of staggered mounds of clay themselves. In my home, I cherish all of my Italian terra-cotta clay pots for the ancient earth they symbolize: Some are festive and painted like frescoes; others are left beautifully naked.

Italy made the artisan noble. Renaissance Italy gave rise to a class of artisan workshops and studios the world had never seen before; today, these craft disciplines are still accorded respect. There are still metal workers in Brescia and ceramists in Tuscany. There is still painted furniture from Umbria and glass from Murano and Venice. The native sense of place has not been milled away by time or imported tastes; rather, it has been raised up as the elemental parent of a great craft tradition that is, as ever, linked to the land that harbors it.

2

Learning to See

Developing

In the Zona home, learning to see is the way to develop a personal aesthetic—a value system that defines one's own sense of beauty, grace, and comfort. In turning a critical eye on everything from one's architecture to the array of one's furnishings, an aesthetic is built in any environment by selecting those core elements that inspire us to harmonize in design: texture, color, form, sense-identity. ¶ Seeking out the beautiful in each adorning object, and in each surface begging adornment, is always the starting point for developing an aesthetic. Formally, beauty is a wholly subjective matter; yet the deepest and most universal reaction to beauty—to be moved beyond the critical to an emotional level of inspiration—is what I call "learning to see." Since beauty crystallizes readily in physical objects, as opposed to the memory of a breathtaking sunset or a masterfully performed symphony, we can always rely on the collected materials in our home environment as symbols of an evolving aesthetic experience. ¶ My friend Joshua Baer, an art dealer from Santa Fe, recently offered me a good explanation of why we seek out beauty in the objects surrounding us: "The eye has an appetite for objects of fascination. Everyone likes to walk into a room, see an amazing object and say, 'How can anything be that beautiful?' To qualify as an object of fascination, an object must *cast a spell. Many things are beautiful, but not all beautiful things are capable of holding people spellbound. In order to do that, the object must possess enigmatic qualities. It must challenge the senses, especially the sense of sight, and then take the eye beyond the act of seeing."* ❡ *At Zona, my aesthetic ensures that all objects entering my environment have that profound, enigmatic significance. Creating a well-formed home goes hand-in-hand with the number of beautiful elements we can collect or unveil as we pass along the arc of our lives.* ❡ *Since the early days of developing my own style and taste, I have practiced "learning to see" to make my own space breathe with a combustible mix of information and energy. In this chapter, we'll examine in depth the primary systems you can culti-vate to retool your own home aesthetic: your architecture, your senses, and your material possessions. First, though, I'd like to share some of the principles I've adopted that serve as guideposts to the practice of "learning to see" itself.*

Aesthetics

Atmosphere

Creating atmosphere at home can enable you to communicate something about your heritage, your passion for collecting, your love of family—something specifically about you. It is an essential aspect of the Zona home. The creation of atmosphere, sparking curiosity and enchantment on the part of a visitor, is a practice I find both rewarding and fun. An engaging atmosphere you light an object of beauty or by the music you play.

The relaxed but stimulating atmosphere that many people associate with Zona requires concentration and discipline, and is actually achieved by maintaining a very controlled structure. Of course, we have people visiting all day long, and the pace of change is much quicker than in residential and personal space. Yet the principles of comfort

sets the stage for people to come together and share quality time. I know I deepen my connection to people when I create an experience that informs them and enables them to feel more closely related to who I am. When atmosphere is practiced daily, a space will begin to develop a sense of age, a true patina from caring. A space becomes recognizably yours by the signature of scent in your rooms or by the way are very much the same. It is an amazing paradox that in order to create an atmosphere that feels casual (which in turn tends to make people feel more comfortable), you have to maintain formality and order in your environment. The key to generating atmosphere at home is learning to see creative ways to elevate the formality without losing your sense of spontaneity or play.

HOW TO | Create Atmosphere and Mood

We've put together this list of simple things you can do to create atmosphere and mood at home and to inspire more lively interplay between your space and your family or guests. Use this as a springboard to come up with your own ways to maintain order and warmth, and remember to test your activities against the emotional and practical missions of your household.

LIGHTING IS KEY TO A COMFORTABLE INTERIOR. Candlelight guarantees atmosphere. Don't be afraid to use less light in a room in the evening—it keeps your interior in tune with the outdoors, and the dark play of shadows creates mood. Make sure to maintain a slight amount of ambient light in rooms other than the one you're in. This produces an immediate lived-in quality when you move from one room to another and is actually conducive to conservation as it eliminates the jarring effect of immediately turning on the overhead light in a dark room.

SELECT SEVERAL BOOKS THAT COMPLEMENT YOUR MOOD AND PLACE THEM ON YOUR COFFEE TABLE. Never leave newspapers and magazines around, and always find a special hiding place for personal mail. It's also wonderful to make available some old-fashioned games like backgammon, cards, or dominoes. These games are often beautiful

artifacts as well, worthy of displaying, and invite immediate group participation.

FLOWERS ALWAYS BRING FOCUS AND COLOR TO A ROOM, BUT TRY TO KEEP THEM IN PERSPECTIVE. If you can make flowers less formal—maybe a single sunflower here or a bundle of thistle there—you'll be more likely to bring them home on a regular basis. Making flowers a part of your regular routine will be a gift to your home and give a lift to otherwise unadorned days. Remember to look for things that are in season and locally grown; these criteria underline your sense of place and make foreign or exotic elements even more special.

BALANCE FLOWERS AND, OF COURSE, PLANTS WITH BOWLS OF OTHER NATURAL DRIED ELEMENTS. Use dried fruits and herbs or stones and colored glass. Even dried beans and lentils, rice, and other foodstuffs like rock salt and whole peppercorns are great. Everyone loves to connect with tactile elements. The texture provided by these decorative elements really helps dimensionalize your space and invites an interaction with all the surfaces of your rooms. Using such commonplace materials in an unexpected, aesthetic way also limbers and cultivates your eye and helps you pay attention to detail.

SCENT IN GENERAL EVOKES SUBLIMINAL RESPONSES, AND AS SUCH SHOULD LINGER IN THE BACKGROUND OF A ROOM. It's best to get into a routine of scenting your space at regular intervals, so that the echo of a fragrance remains from day to day and becomes woven into the atmosphere of a room. Keep the air in your space fresh and aromatic. Make sure to keep windows open as much as possible. Use fans to create crosscurrents in hot weather so you can turn off the air-conditioning at least some of the time and natural-

ize the climate. If you are entertaining, take care to scent well before your guests arrive. Use a mixture of things—layer with candles, potpourri, room essences, and misters. Bathrooms deserve special attention: The burning of small scented votive candles is ideal for creating immediate luxury and intimacy.

BACKGROUND MUSIC HELPS SET TONE AND BALANCE IN A SPACE. Stay active in your musical playlist. The best way to develop a sense of music is to listen to music. Practice variety and strive for a broadened perspective. Special emphasis should be placed on the growing assortment of ethnic and instrumental recordings from different countries. Jazz is classic. If your own interest is limited, find a friend who likes to make mixes. Also, try to substitute music for television whenever you can. You will be delighted by the heightened level of good conversation that music can induce and will be soothed in contemplative times spent away from the false lull of packaged sound bites.

TAKE TIME TO CELEBRATE EVEN SIMPLE MOMENTS. Bring out a pair of pretty china teacups and buy some little cakes to share with a friend or family member you see all the time. Make weekend breakfast with your kids a festive affair. Gather together a selection of toasting glasses, old and new, to make the sharing of a glass of wine special. Find one wine glass that you really like and keep it for yourself. Always buy one special thing at the grocery store that isn't essential: a certain imported brand of cocoa, an exotic spice you don't normally use, your favorite brand of cookies or cereal from childhood. All these activities raise up the ordinary and make home a special place to be all the time.

Point of View

Another aspect of creating a personal aesthetic is realizing a point of view with material possessions, based on the goals of your space. When you introduce objects into the picture of home, you have to take care that each one will satisfy a set of needs both formal and functional. The cultivation of an eye requires that you look at many objects and absorb what each one has to offer without losing sight of your own circumstances and needs. Seeing has to do with a way of looking at space, color, texture, and pattern—the elements of every object.

Point of view is critical when gathering information about an object. For example, if I am going out to look for a dining room table and chairs, I am working to visualize what my ideal would be, stylistically. In addition, I know how many people I want to accommodate; I know my family's dining routines; I have evaluated how much entertaining I really do in a year. I have taken the time to review the proportions of my space. I am prepared to speak clearly about the details. All this groundwork and context sets me free to explore and discover. This is the basis of how I see any object today.

The Tale of the Blue Pie Safe

"YOU ARE BEGINNING TO CULTIVATE YOUR
EYE WHEN YOU LOOK AT AN OBJECT AND FEEL ITS ENERGY.
IT IS A PROCESS, AN EVOLUTION THAT IS STRENGTHENED
BY TRIAL AND ERROR OVER TIME."

—LOUIS SAGAR

I remember one time, a few years back, I was lined up for early buying at a well known antiques fair. Have you ever been to a country antique show early in the morning? Well, it was before dawn, and all these people were running around drinking bad coffee and searching for treasures, but you could barely see a thing. It was still too dark. I noticed a beautiful blue pie safe right off the bat, studied it for a few moments and moved on. The fields were full of wonderful things, and I had just entered the fair, but I kept returning in my mind to the aged tin and faded color of that pie safe.

I came back around to the dealer about an hour or so later, whereupon I noticed that the pie safe was not as blue as I had thought. I was disappointed at first. It had more colors than blue, but I still liked the form and proportions. The dealer said the pie safe was from Indiana. I asked him some other questions and left again. I liked the soft edges of the piece. I noted its original iron door latch. I thought about the aroma of fresh baked pies that emanated from it in the past. I wondered how old it was and who had built it. I kept moving, but still, I could not get that pie safe off my mind.

I went back to the dealer again a little later. This time, I really examined the piece—opened its doors, looked at its back, checked the joints and shelves. Finally I ran my hands over the punctured tin patterns. The panels were worn and authentic. By this time in the morning the sun was shining, and I noticed that where the paint was cracked and chipped, traces of green and even the original pine were revealed. This particular pie safe had an unusually primitive feeling to it. Hitting upon this sensibility determined for me what I loved about the piece, and helped me decide to buy it.

You are beginning to cultivate your eye when you look at an object and feel its energy. It is a process, an evolution that is strengthened by trial and error over time. When well practiced, your eye can become an essential guide to how you design and decorate your home. It will help you create atmosphere and sustain a cohesive style throughout your environment. It will have a magical impact on your family and friends when they come to visit. Through these means of evaluating and adapting your interior space, you will become ever clearer on the personal meaning of home and settle into a new level of enjoyment and confidence that your space is serving you well. This is the ambition behind learning to see.

ORIGINAL INDIANA TIN PIE SAFE, CIRCA 1920, FROM MY PRIVATE COLLECTION.

The Structure of Shelter

In developing our home aesthetic, we tune in first to the space itself. It is important to be attentive to the structure and layout of your personal space. We should give ourselves the assignment of envisioning our space raw: learning the flow of its lines; deciphering which aspects of the construction need to be conditioned or rehabilitated; taking into account and focusing on its best

attributes. For example, one of the most valuable lessons I have learned from my experience at Zona is how to capitalize on a space's best features. In my case, Zona's location boasted great height and light. I have always been grateful for the natural light that comes into our SoHo store from above. The skylights have had an unusually strong impact on making our space feel like home. So has the height of our ceilings. Height often gives people an immediate sense of mobility, and produces a feeling of soaring space even if the floor area is narrow or constricted. Small or large, humble or grand, size has little bearing on the ultimate construction of a home.

OPPOSITE: A WOODEN SKELETAL FRAMEWORK BEING PREPARED FOR ITS SKIN, BAKERSFIELD, CALIFORNIA.

HOW TO | Critique Architectural Shelter

The cultivated eye is always seeking unity and cohesion between positives and negatives. You will learn to see by studying how the structural and decorative components of your home come together. Focus your eye on identifying the special features of your home so that you can highlight and enhance them. Examine the weaker aspects of your home and explore how to make them less troublesome. When you understand and can improve on the details, you will carry off your room settings with greater sensitivity and confidence.

START YOUR CRITIQUE BY TAKING A WALK THROUGH YOUR SPACE WITHOUT THE BENEFIT OF ARTIFICIAL LIGHTING. Do this once in daylight and once in the evening. Take note of how much sunlight each of your rooms gets and how much illumination each needs in the absence of natural light. Pay attention to which rooms you spend the most time in after dark, as they require the most critical lighting.

Activate all of your senses to the job of looking and simply make note of the problem areas you find along the way.

MAKE A QUICK SCAN OF EACH WALL FROM TOP TO BOTTOM, THE WAY YOU WOULD LOOK AT YOURSELF IN THE MIRROR. This will help you gauge the proportions of your space in one broad stroke, and will keep architectural details in the context of the length, width, and depth they're built into.

LOOK FOR THE NATURAL PATHWAYS IN YOUR HOME. Determine the flow of movement in your home that help keeps the space unified. Make note of the overall shape and dimension of your home. Does the division of space provide a good balance between the need for privacy and the desire for openness? Map out your raw space, or use a copy of your blueprint, and mark down any areas that feel constrained or bottlenecked, gathering points that do not feel centered, spaces that are underutilized. Your initial assessment of personal space should concentrate on the basics.

Leave decorative issues, such as paint, pattern, texture, and furnishings until later on.

THE NEXT STEP IS TO DECONSTRUCT YOUR SPACE INTO ELEMENTS: WINDOWS, DOORS, ARCHWAYS, STAIRWELLS, FLOORS, WALLS, CORNERS. Evaluate which features display extra character and take note of them: a parquet floor, a wainscoted wall, a timbered ceiling. At the same time, take stock of poorly conceived or generic elements that you can change or divert attention from. Keep the measurements of these features in a notebook so that if you have occasion to renovate, you have all the information you need when you start looking for replacement fixtures and hardware.

MOVE TO A REVIEW OF YOUR SPACE ROOM BY ROOM. Make a list of the standard activities you perform in the different rooms of your home, and prepare a graph showing the amount of time you spend in each one. Be honest with yourself about the way you use your home and dedicate space according to your own personal preferences and routines. Change your floor plan around so that you dedicate the best architectural space to your favorite activities, even if that means reinterpreting rooms for unusual uses.

FINALLY, AFTER LOOKING AT THE STRUCTURAL AND SPATIAL DETAILS OF YOUR SPACE, LOOK FOR THE PURELY DECO-

RATIVE ONES. For example, in an old house pay attention to details like old glass panes in your windows and grain painting on doors. Take note of a beautifully carved mantel—that can become the centerpiece of a room. Use the themes of your architecture as a base for decorating, either as a complement or a counterpoint to your interior furnishings. Once you've laid this true map of your space over your initial architectural blueprint, you are on your way to reclaiming your home from misuse and missed design opportunities, all from the ground up.

Here are some examples of other questions you may find helpful to ask while you are critiquing your space:

1. In which room do friends and family tend to gather?

2. Where are you eating your meals—in the kitchen, in the dining room, or perhaps on a coffee table in front of the TV?

3. How long will you be living in this space? Will your needs and lifestyle be the same five years from now?

4. How much architectural and spatial change is required in your home to achieve your goals and support your needs?

5. How many of the desired changes in your home can be achieved through interior design and decoration?

6. What are the special work and living routines of all the different members of your family?

The Architecture

·

After evaluating what works and what needs work in the composition of your architectural space, here are some ideas to get you started bonding the basic structural features of your home to the flow of your furnishings and routines.

WINDOWS

Among friends who work at home we've found that windows should be generously spent on work space. The strain of spending hours bent over paperwork or craft, or looking at the electronic window of a computer screen, is soothed simply by having sunlight stream into the work area. In these solitary spaces, it's a relief to hear the rain pelting against the glass in a spring downpour or the whirling of a fan propped in the window frame to allow the air to circulate.

When you don't want to face the world outside, or let it see in, then windows can provide the visual rhythm of curtains or shades. We especially love wooden blinds: louvered, they still let in diffused light, and offer an opaque, natural texture that blends gracefully with all manner of decor. We take our cue with blinds from outdoor shutters; if we want to give the illusion of a window opening onto a view, we can create a false window by hanging old barn shutters on the wall. You can also try changing your window treatments with the seasons, lightening up the materials and colors in warmer weather and using heavier, opaque shades in the cold months.

Windows also provide our homes with the best intermediate step between outdoors and indoors. Trailing ivy across the window screen, window boxes filled with flowers, weather and scent and sound being blown inside, remind us of nature's proximity and always help us naturalize our living space. If you are an avid cook without a viable garden plot, try growing your favorite herbs in your window boxes instead of flowers.

WINDOWS LOOKING OUT OVER A SCULPTURAL MASS OF TIN ROOFING FIND GRACEFUL NEIGHBORS ACROSS THE WAY IN THIS (SOHO, PARIS) SETTING.

A VINTAGE DOOR CREATES DRAMA IN THE ENTRYWAY OF ANY ROOM AND SETS THE TONE FOR THE ARCHITECTURAL DETAIL THROUGHOUT THE SPACE.

DOORS

Doors should be looked at with respect to the important acts of entry and exit. The front door and entry should be treated as a microcosm of the entire home within, sending an immediate message of welcome and comfort with the help of good lighting, wreaths and other natural materials, and storage for coats, shoes, keys, and other baggage from the outside world.

Interior doors can get a makeover too. One of our favorite examples of good architectural renovation is to use vintage doors all throughout a space as replacements for those standard slim-width doors, which are so plain and barely ever block out external noise. Get to know your local architectural salvage dealers, and let them help you find the perfect doors to fit in your space. Often you can have an old door cut down to size. Architectural salvage houses are also great places to find interesting old doorknobs and other fixtures, if replacing the door in its entirety just isn't an option.

Another good choice is to find doors made out of uncommon materials, such as sandblasted steel and treated metals. And if you want to open up a space visually without losing the privacy of a closed door, glass-paned French doors are a great option. French doors are often one of the last graceful features left in place in old apartments. Make the most of them when you have them by painting the trim an accent color and hanging curtains of luxurious silk or linen on one side for privacy.

"IF ONE WERE TO GIVE AN ACCOUNT OF ALL THE DOORS ONE HAS CLOSED AND OPENED, OF ALL THE DOORS ONE WOULD LIKE TO RE-OPEN, ONE WOULD HAVE TO TELL THE STORY OF AN ENTIRE LIFE."

—GASTON BACHELARD

FROM A FULLY DEVELOPED SETTING FOR ANTIQUES TO AN EXERCISE IN SPARE DECOR, A COMPLETE TREATMENT FOR
THE STAIRS IN YOUR HOME WILL HELP ESTABLISH AND CARRY A SENSE OF STYLE FROM ONE FLOOR TO ANOTHER.

STAIRWAYS

Moving between floors allows us to cultivate different levels of intimacy at home. Stairs can serve that passage well when treated like a vertical hallway. Start with the stairwell itself. If the materials and fabrication are beautiful, as they often are, play them up by leaving them alone. This will draw the eye in to the beautiful curve of wrought iron or the detailed carving of heavy wood. Architectural salvage houses are again great resources for finding interesting finials and turned posts to spruce up a plain staircase.

If the stairs show the wear and tear of years of foot traffic, you can highlight the effect rather than cover it up by giving the steps a serious coat of oil or wax. The patina of use is often extremely beautiful, especially in old houses. Other options for your steps include carpet runners—try using fragments of kilims, all in the same color family but with different patterns every few steps—or a good coat of paint. Try painting your stairwell in a deep, saturated color to accentuate its form, or play with a graphic pattern of parquet squares using stencils.

The stairwell also provides us with an expanse of wall we don't often have anywhere else in our home. Since we move up and down the stairs with extreme frequency and speed, we suggest filling that wall space with visual elements—framed art, family photos, even a distinct wash of color.

Textures

You can decorate far more comprehensively if you really count your wall space as usable square footage. Start with the color you paint your periphery. You might be interested in making a statement with clean white walls, yet you still have to do your homework: There are hundreds of white tints from which to choose. Take time before you paint to test out several different base colors—cool whites, linen whites, warm whites—and make note of how the available light bounces off or is absorbed into the walls. This will help you choose the white that is best suited to your environment. Even if you plan to use a lot of color on your walls, always start your paint selection with the white you like and use it as a springboard to choose the right tones from your color palette.

At Zona, we became known early on for changing the tonal range of our walls seasonally. We found that tinting our walls to accommodate the changing light outside helped brighten everything we put up. At home, repainting at regular intervals may not be feasible, so we recommend starting with a warm, light palette. Washing a wall with successive layers of diluted pigment adds tremendous texture, and softens the light as it hits and bounces off all the objects in a room. You can also wallpaper, stencil, or texture your walls to set the tone and create cohesion with your furnishings.

Hang art, photography, or textiles to add vertical action to a room. Collections, or series of objects hung in a line or in squares, add three-dimensionality to a space and create context for the furniture placed underneath.

CORNERS

Corners are constructed for single habitation and provide an intimate counterpoint to a home's open spaces. We even create corners without walls—by setting a lone rocking chair next to a fireplace or by piling a bunch of pillows to lounge against while reading the paper in bed on Sunday morning.

Corners don't have to be wasted space. Painting the molding around the floorboards an accent color draws the eye around the perimeter of a room and provides a perfect stage for a small chair or pedestaled object of beauty. Setting furniture on a diagonal in a corner is a way to create a curve of space in a room.

If one of the attributes of your space is high ceilings, try painting an accent color or stencil a strip of pattern around the top of the walls, or blur the lines altogether between ceiling and wall with textural painting, to produce an arching effect in your space. Or apply gilding to any architectural molding you have. This practice adds immediate elegance to a room.

STUDYING VARIOUS ARCHITECTURAL SURFACES IN ISOLATION PROVIDES GREAT INSPIRATION FOR TEXTURE IN THE HOME: THE MOTTLED EFFECT OF LAYERS OF PAINT ON WOOD; THE REPEATING CURVE OF CORRUGATED SHEET METAL; THE ECHO OF ROMANTIC FLORETS IN A FADED STENCIL. ALL OF THESE EXAMPLES ARE SOURCES FOR TEXTURES CREATED OUT OF BOTH COLOR AND PATTERN.

The Principles of Feng Shui

"TO ENHANCE YOUR ABILITY TO MOVE FORWARD,
MOVE TWENTY-SEVEN OBJECTS IN YOUR
HOME WHICH HAVE NOT BEEN MOVED IN THE LAST
YEAR. TO CULTIVATE GOOD LUCK, PLACE
FLOWERS IN THE BEDROOM, STUDY, AND KITCHEN."

—Louis Sagar

Feng shui is an ancient practice from China that is dedicated to the study of energy, or "chi," as it relates to physical environments. Practitioners of this discipline determine and adjust energy affecting people, space, and natural landscapes. Having a rudimentary understanding of the principles of feng shui can help you assess the way energy flows through your household. We asked our friend David Cho, of the American Feng Shui Institute, to give us a fundamental introduction to this traditional practice.

Throughout ancient China, classical feng shui was a closely guarded discipline used as a tool to ensure the good health, wealth, and power of the imperial dynasties. The keepers of this secret knowledge were the feng shui masters, the highly respected scientists and astronomers who were charged with sustaining the good fortune and prosperity of the royal court.

The practice of feng shui enlightens, harmonizes, and improves lives by identifying and orchestrating the relationships and natural rhythms of energy that affect us daily.

Here are some basic guidelines for creating more auspicious and abundant living and work spaces:

Good energy thrives in positive environments. Surround yourself with people and objects that invigorate.

Place trust in your five senses to create beautiful and dynamic settings. Balance elements of light with dark; soft with hard; smooth with rough; yin with yang.

Avoid sleeping or working under ceiling beams or in the energy path of a doorway. The turbulence of the chi will interrupt your peace of mind or concentration, and eventually cause health problems or feelings of instability.

Rounded corners and soft curves promote the positive flow of energy. Conversely, sharp corners and angled shapes disrupt its natural rhythms and will add to unwanted chaos and confusion.

Every house has unique energy characteristics, so be wary of feng shui systems that offer fixed solutions. The prescribed remedies may actually do more harm than good.

Be wise, be happy, and be like a Chinese emperor. Apply feng shui to your personal universe!

OPPOSITE: A THOUGHTFUL ARRANGEMENT OF THESE RUSTIC HICKORY CHAIRS STIMULATES A SENSE OF BALANCE IN THE HOME.

A Harbor for Nature

We have long been conditioned to construct homes that cleanly partition outdoors from indoors. Now, as home has become a renewed territory to explore, we must make it a harbor for the celebration of nature. This is how we can activate our senses to import the experience of the natural from outside to inside.

The experience of the outdoors can contribute meaningfully to the interior style of our homes. For example, when I present a collection of vintage fly-fishing baskets on a wall in my living room, I am reminded of being out on the river, invigorated by the cold morning air, and focused on chilly streams moving with trout. When I display a handful of smooth rocks and pebbles gathered during an afternoon walk along the beach, I extend the enjoyment of that outdoor experience. I am encouraged to journey outdoors again. The goal here is to begin minimizing the distance between our experiences out in the world and our life at home.

A COLLECTION OF VINTAGE CREEL BASKETS HANDSOMELY REPRESENTS A FAVORITE OUTDOOR ACTIVITY—FLY FISHING—WITHIN THE HOME.

A Drive to the Countryside

I recall a time when my budget for flowers at Zona was extremely tight. It was around Thanksgiving, a holiday weekend, and I anticipated good traffic in my store. I wanted the space to feel in touch with the harvest. I had a secondhand station wagon at the time, and I took an early morning drive to the western part of New Jersey. I came upon a park with large mounds of leaves—leaves with bursts of orange and red and yellow and brown. I loaded up the back of my wagon with as many leaves, branches, and bundles of twigs as I could gather. When I returned to the store, I filled some baskets in the windows with the mounds of leaves. Then I carefully placed the twigs and branches in sculptural piles all around the rest of the space. I put some above an old cupboard and I placed an assortment of twigs in between items on shelves. ¶   Somehow, the new context for the leaves, branches, and twigs provided them with renewed color and warmth. These were common textural elements gathered at a time of year when they were full of pride, in the prime of their color. Since that time, I have always enjoyed the process of simply walking and gathering natural elements from the countryside, to commemorate the change of season within my space.

HOW TO | Gather Natural Materials for the Home

1. Select a backpack that has expandable space and fits comfortably on your back.

2. Pack up several plastic containers, a number of large garbage bags, old newspapers, and scotch tape. Some shopping bags are also helpful. A small pair of pruning shears is essential. If you have binoculars and a magnifying glass, bring those along as well.

3. The romantics will always carry their favorite books of poems in their back pocket. If that's not for you, bring along a reference book or two instead so that you can learn to identify the species of plants and trees and birds you will encounter.

4. A pen and notebook are essential for jotting down flashes, dreams, and brainstorms. Take a stab at sketching some of the flora you see, or do some rubbings with newsprint and a soft pencil. Record the information you've learned about different trees and plants, and trace the silhouettes of your favorite elements. Press sample leaves and petals in the book for safekeeping.

5. Think about where you want to walk. Don't shy away from planning day trips to larger patches of nature, like the beach or a forest preserve. Taking a long hike on a wilderness trail will often provide you with examples of habitats that sustain diverse and pleasingly foreign plant life.

6. After you pick your walking route, open your eyes. Look up. Look for the life of everything around you. Focus especially on things you don't immediately recognize, or on colors you find unusual. Whatever stimulates you, try to gather it: a stone, a twig, a leaf, mounds of sand, even the earth itself. Some elements are fine alone, others are lovely in groupings, and still others look good in abundance. Use your magnifying glass to enjoy a close-up look at anything small.

7. When you get back home, lay your collection on a coffee or dining room table. Notice how the textures and colors seem to become more intense when they are seen out of context.

8. Pull out your favorite bowls, baskets, or plates. Find the right home for each of the elements you have found.

9. Enjoy the process. Have fun. Remember that as soon as your elements age or wither, you can go outside and gather new ones!

Sanctuary for the Senses

"HOME IS A SHRINE, IN WHICH TO
CELEBRATE A NATURAL, TEXTURAL, AND ELEMENTAL
RELATIONSHIP TO NATURE."

—Louis Sagar

Zona's home-making aesthetic requires that we stay centered on a high plane of sense awareness. To keep the senses limber, they need to be flexed and stretched. This determines the acuteness of our response to the aroma of chicken soup on the stove or the rich color of tulips just gathered from the garden. Our senses pick up the festive air of the holiday season, the warmth of a crackling fire, the delectable flavors of a summer salad and sunset barbecue, and turn these phenomena into experience. They are the tools that guide us in how we respond to our surroundings. When we have the system of our senses activated, we know how to feel at home.

The most embracing and memorable environments I have visited have stimulated all of my senses at once. I've experienced a sort of total harmony in such places that put me at ease. For example, a visit to a Tuscan vineyard on an autumn morning before the harvest is an awesome event. Astounding visual beauty is complemented by the subtle scent of the grapes, full and rich. You can almost hear the vines singing in the light breeze; you can imagine the taste and texture of the wine. Or, take for instance a visit to a Balinese temple for a ceremonial evening of dancing. The intensity of color in the costumes and decorations is overwhelming, the pungent scent of incense envelops everything, the sounds of music and movement create an amplified pulse in the air. Tastes of honey and cakes add to the sensory delight. Experiences like these, which displayed a completely integrated sensual atmosphere, have motivated me to find new ways to bring the sensory landscape into my own space. Let's look at how to harness each sense individually to elevate and stimulate our ambient experience of home.

OPPOSITE: AN ASSORTMENT OF BOTANICAL ELEMENTS, DELICATELY PLACED ON HAND-MADE PAPERS, CREATES A TACTILE
AND SENSORIAL ASSEMBLAGE.

Sight

"THE SENSES DON'T JUST MAKE SENSE OF
LIFE IN BOLD OR SUBTLE ACTS OF CLARITY, THEY TEAR
REALITY APART INTO VIBRANT MORSELS AND
REASSEMBLE THEM INTO A MEANINGFUL PATTERN."

—DIANE ACKERMAN

The most amazing thing about our power of sight is that we can visualize the world with our eyes opened or closed. We perceive shapes, movement, tone. Sight gives us orientation. We distinguish distance from proximity; we measure our relative scale against other objects as with no other sense.

At home, our eye is cultivated by the two primary effects of vision: light and color. Light has a lot to do with how we perceive color. We have to be sensitive to the vagaries of light at home, the shifting mood from natural illumination to electric light as day turns to night, the seasonal withering of daylight hours, the transition from yellow and gold to gray and blue as temperature alters the air. One essential we always recommend for any room is an ambient light source, like a floor lamp with a filtered shade (mica and blown glass are two of our favorites). The light emanating from this type of source facilitates a human scale in proportion to the space, and softens any overhead lighting we may be required to employ. Louvered shades are also good bets for creating ambient light, allowing shadowplay on the walls to create texture in a room with the help of a little diffused sunlight. Dimmers are always important so that we can adjust overhead lighting to keep it in accordance with a room's mood. Light gives a space its theatricality.

Candlelight furnishes us with a sense of intimacy and history—after all, it's not been that long since people illuminated all of their darkened hours at home with candles. We contract light to its smallest glowing point when we use candles; we celebrate shadow and revealed form. But with candles we can exploit color as well, for as any wax burns, it gives off a translucent shimmer that is pure visual delight. We always keep a wide array of tinted candles at home and use them to tell the color story of a room.

Color creates an emotional narrative backdrop on the stage of a home. You can derive your palette of home colors from any inspirational source. A trip to the Mediterranean may translate into a particular translucent sea blue for the tiles in your kitchen; a visit to the circus with your kids might reveal exactly the right red to use as an accent color in their rooms. When working with color, you should embrace the palettes you find yourself drawn to in the outside world. At Zona, we have been deeply inspired by the overlapping earth tones of the Southwest: the almost rosy sand and red clay, the dense clean blue of high mesa sky, the ancient white of adobe and silvery weight of dark pine. This palette is a natural phenomenon. Reproduced in a new context, the earth tones will remain integrated and produce a calming effect.

COLOR AND LIGHT ILLUMINATED THROUGH PANES OF GLASS.

HOW TO | Cultivate Your Sense of Color

Color is very subjective. Rarely do two people respond to the impact of a color in the same way. In recent years, color has become a media event. We find color consultants who advise us on what colors are in vogue for the season. We have others advising on the colors to dress in for success. There are interior designers who tell us what colors our offices should be and in what colors our furniture should be upholstered. And yet, as we listen and follow counsel, we often cloud our own instinctive sense of color. Maintaining your own perspective is important when deciding how and where to use color in your home.

The Zona approach uses color as the background or harmonizing influence in a room. It is very important to keep the background colors simple, with an emphasis on neutrals such as parchment, taupe, ocher, pale yellow, and soft blue-gray. Practice using complementary primary colors through your selection of home furnishings. Fabrics

are especially easy to change as your interior style grows and evolves, and they afford you the opportunity to experiment with pattern and texture as well. When trying to articulate the feel of a room, always start with a summary of color. As you conceive your background palette, and highlight the natural colors of wood, metal, stone, and tile in the architectural detail of your space, you can also start to think about which possessions might anchor a space through color. Possessions and furniture amplify the overall tone of a room.

Shifting ranges of color can be used to great effect in problem areas at home to create or hide spatial divisions where architecture falls short. If you are troubled by a room with low ceilings, you might want to paint all the walls and the ceiling a single pale color, to erase the boundaries of perpendicular planes. Or you might want to play around with washes of light blue pigment on the ceiling to imitate the openness of the sky. To play up the intimacies of a small space, you could choose a darker color for the whole interior of a room. If a change of mood is desired from room to room, try painting different spaces different colors. This won't sacrifice the cohesiveness of your interior plan. Weaving colors together creates dimension in the spectrum of your environment.

EXAMPLES OF COLOR FROM BOTH NATURAL AND ARCHITECTURAL SOURCES CAN BE TRANSLATED INTO A DEFINING THEMATIC FRAMEWORK FOR THE HOME, OR USED SIMPLY AS A WHIMSICAL COUNTERPOINT TO THE FORM OF A FAVORITE PIECE OF FURNITURE, LIKE THIS MANY-DRAWERED APOTHECARY CABINET.

RAINBOWS ARE REDISCOVERED IN THE SATURATED COLORS FOUND IN THE SIGNATURE SWISS CANDLES MADE BY HAND
IN A SMALL WORKSHOP IN THE FARMLANDS JUST OUTSIDE OF ZURICH.

Touch

"TOUCH, BY CLARIFYING AND ADDING TO
THE SHORTHAND OF THE EYES, TEACHES US THAT WE
LIVE IN A THREE-DIMENSIONAL WORLD."

—DIANE ACKERMAN

Every object has a skin or texture. Even air: The feel of a warm breeze in spring or a blast of hot wind from a roaring fire resonates deeply in our sense of touch. We look especially to organic materials—flowers, vegetables, stone, water, wood—when creating our vocabulary of texture in the home. As with a tree outside, the play of crude bark against smooth leaf is echoed in the veiny sheen of a kilim rug on a hardwood floor.

Hard-soft, hot-cold, smooth-rough: Touch works in binary opposites. We feel a tile floor as cool against our bare feet in contrast to the warmth of our woolen socks. Understanding touch in this way is critical to our application of texture in the home. We try to create balance in rooms by allowing both sides of a tactile experience to be present. Rather than repeating a series of positive textures one after one, we alternate positive, negative, positive, negative. This method produces dynamics, and dynamics produce mood.

Take a still life on a coffee table. If you have a table made of old pine boards, you're working off a thick, opaque, rough texture, with lots of pattern inherent in the grain of the wood. So you would want to place objects on that table that have contrasting surfaces—things made of glass or polished metal are good bets. This is why a beautiful collection of shiny brass or pewter candlesticks looks more at home on a wooden mantle than a marble one. Or why nubby placemats help distinguish the flat, cool surface of a glass table from the smooth white china you might entertain with. You can use the rule of contrasting textures to complete pleasing still lifes all around the home.

In the kitchen, a pantry shelf comes to life by taking an assortment of old glass jars and filling them with various grains and beans and spices. The different foodstuffs play off each other in terms of scale—a handful of peppercorns placed against a strawlike bundle of pasta or a heaping pile of flour. What's more, the liquid smoothness of the glass jars acts as a perfect counterpoint to the multiple nubby textures of dry ingredients. Storing food this way also has a practical side: Glass isn't porous, and so keeps moisture out. Glass jars also allow us to see what we've got without opening spouts and lids, creating a more efficient inventory for the busy cook.

At Zona, we are moved to bring as many natural elements as possible inside to create texture. Some we dry and keep around as reminders of other seasons—a bundle of stems hung on a door, a pile of driftwood stored in a corner like sculpture, a collection of organic sponges lining the rim of the bathtub. We make visual potpourri by mixing up a variety of dried elements like pods and cones and twigs. In early spring, we can even create a natural display out of a pile of bulbs before we are ready to plant them.

Some materials suggest the creation of an organic environment to highlight their unusual textures. Try presenting your summer's collection of beach glass or pebbles in a shallow bowl filled with water, so they keep the sheen of just washing up on the shore. Construct a miniature sandbox to show off the treasures your kids collect, or plant a bunch of long branches in a large earthen pot—half tree, half sculpture. Make a perfect autumn centerpiece for the harvest table with an old sap bucket filled to brimming with brightly toned leaves.

THE RUGGED HANDS OF MASTER BLACKSMITH GLEN GILMORE FROM BRASSTOWN, NORTH CAROLINA.

HOW TO | Make Visual Potpourri

"THE FINEST RECIPES FOR POTPOURRI COMPLEMENT
THE INGREDIENTS WITH A TOUCH OF THE
UNEXPECTED, AND A DASH OF PERSONAL CHARM."

—LOUIS SAGAR

The making of a visual potpourri is achieved by bringing a unique mix of natural elements together, emphasizing the tactile in a blend of elements.

1. Practice being thematic. A seasonal or environmental reference point is most important. Use materials that are bountiful in the area where you live, some of which you might even gather yourself.

2. Create a core assortment of elements. For example, here is a short list of my favorite potpourri ingredients (see box at right).

3. Store your elements in containers, like paints in jars or spices in your kitchen.

4. Visual potpourri bowls can be large or small, old or new. Many people prefer using wooden bowls for tone and texture, but glass and ceramic are fine too, especially if they're tinted. Collect bowls to use in display, and store them on a shelf like a collection.

5. Making visual potpourri is like making a salad. Care must be taken to mix large ingredients with smaller ones. The color or shape of one element should enhance that of the others. Layering is vital. Sometimes I like to anchor the mix with a piece of cloth, like an old napkin, or a cut-up piece of flannel from an old shirt. This gives me some background off which to work. Try not to use too many elements. Being simple is often better. The fun is in both the experimenting and the constant opportunity for change.

OPPOSITE: A SERIES OF TEXTURAL ELEMENTS DEPICTS EXAMPLES OF INGREDIENTS USED TO MAKE VISUAL POTPOURRI. TOP LEFT, A BOWL OF DRIED FRUITS; MIDDLE LEFT, A BOWL OF STONE CALENDAR EGGS; LOWER LEFT, AN ASSEMBLAGE OF NATURAL ROSE CEDAR CONES; TOP RIGHT, A BASKET OF GATHERED DRIFTWOOD; MIDDLE RIGHT, COLORFUL DRIED FLORAL ELEMENTS; LOWER RIGHT, A MASON JAR OF VINTAGE BUTTONS; CENTER, A GROUPING OF MOUNTAIN RIVER STONES.

ELEMENTS

stones and pebbles

crystals

nuts

seeds and pods

driftwood

bark

twigs and branches

seasonal fruits that have a long shelf life (I love coconuts)

hand-made papers cut up into small pieces

shells, starfish, and beach glass

bones and fossils

bits of vintage silk, old cottons, and ribbons (I love vintage bandannas and old handkerchiefs)

USE A PANTRY SHELF TO DISPLAY OLIVE OILS, VINEGARS, SPICES, SEASONINGS, AND WALL ELEMENTS.

Taste

Taste is the most social of senses. We enjoy its benefits with others. The experience of food, especially at home, encourages us to be intimate with the environment in which we dine. It is the taste of the homemade that keeps us going back to the kitchen: the taste of turkey at a holiday feast, the taste of honey on a slice of apple, or of sweet corn served at the peak of summer. We savor and remember all these flavors, storing them at home until we can taste them again.

Tasting food or drink occupies in many ways the most sophisticated stage of sensory perception, and that's why we remember flavors so well. Taste involves all the other senses: smell, texture, and to lesser degrees, even sight and hearing. What we taste is the overlayer, the fusion, of all these elements. We might remember the taste of a perfect ripe tomato when we run cold water over any vegetable in the sink during late summer; or, we can evoke memories of every peanut butter and jelly sandwich we ate when we were kids by keeping a sentinel jar of peanut butter on a shelf in the pantry.

Decorating a home with representatives of taste helps deepen respect for the gift of good food. At home, we like to keep a collection of different olive oils—some to infuse with other flavors if we are motivated and others for their distinctive packaging. We line them up behind our stove or even place them on the sideboard in the dining area for decoration. We lay out a still life of fruits and cheeses or a basket brimming with different colored vegetables in the center of the table instead of filling the space with a vase with flowers. We eat primarily out of bowls—stacked sculpturally for serving, on the table as well—large, wide bowls for heaping servings of pasta, rice, or salad. We like to col-

FUNCTIONAL AREAS OF OUR HOMES PROVIDE FOR A CHANGING STILL LIFE.

lect ceramic bowls of all sizes and display them on high shelves in the kitchen. Then, whenever we need one, we have a mixing or serving bowl at hand.

At Zona we have long looked abroad for models of both food preparation and regional food production. Now, as organic farming is growing more and more prevalent in this country, it's becoming easier here to buy fresh, natural food for the home table. The benefits are many. We are taking better care of the earth, we buy less (and waste less) when the ingredients we need are readily available, and the food tastes better. In creating a sanctuary for taste at home, we encourage the use of fresh ingredients, both for display and for consumption, whenever possible. One of our favorite things to do with fresh herbs, for example, is to bundle up small bouquets of different cooking blends and display them until they're used: One bundle might contain basil, sage, thyme, and oregano; another might hold mint, parsley, and rosemary.

Taste finds a special nostalgia with sweets. A cultivated love of sugar deserves its own collection of playful relics. A wonderful way to pay tribute to sweets, without necessarily consuming as many of them as we used to, is to collect vintage regional soda bottles or old candy and cocoa tins. Even old candy wrappers—as a sort of visual memoir, it's fun to frame the wrapper of your favorite childhood candy bar. We remember how things taste for a long, long time, so an honorary catalyst for those sweet sense memories can be a fitting substitute for the real thing.

Zona has always sold great homemade foodstuffs that elevate the importance of taste. We appreciate, especially at holiday time, that when you have a limited amount of something homemade, it's seen as extra special because you can't get more of it right away. When you run out, it's over—at least until next year. In the spirit of keeping the homemade around all year long, we try to make time to prepare our favorite treats—jams, cookies, pies, bread—in our own kitchen at least once a season. There is no greater way to share the feeling of home with family and friends than to serve up a specialty of the house.

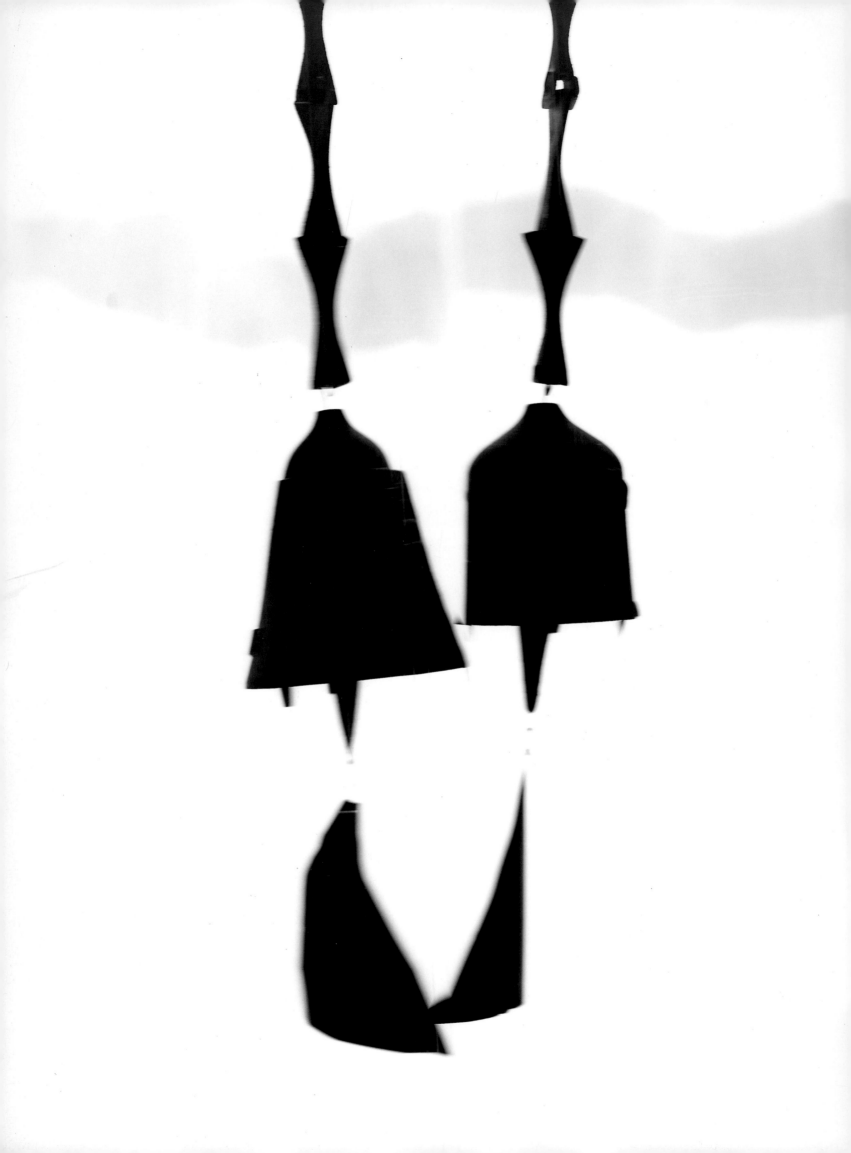

Sound

"WE LEARN THAT SOUND CAN BE BEST
HONORED WHEN WE ATTUNE TO IT IN A VERY DIMINISHED
AND PURIFIED STATE. WITH SOUND, LESS IS OFTEN MORE."

—LOUIS SAGAR

The most subliminal of senses, sound is a constant presence, even if we are almost unaware of it. Sound is distinguished more by the hush of listening than the immediacy of hearing. If we can listen for the subtle, organic soundscape in our homes, we will learn how to be more in tune with the natural flow of our surroundings.

Bringing an echo of the outdoors inside is a good way to restore the balance between organic and amplified sound. For example, windows serve as mediators of sound as much as light: They let in the soothing hush of wind and falling rain, of almost silent snowfall, of birds marking daylight, and the whoosh of passing laughter as people walk by. In moments of solitude and silence, we become aware of these ambient pulses. We can construct lures of sorts to encourage the sweeter sounds to move in close and mute the less pleasant tones trying to work their way inside.

A good example of this sort of sound screen is a birdhouse. As an object itself, it makes no sound; however, the birds it will attract will provide a natural singsong melody throughout even the coldest winter days. We are reminded through this music of our proximity to nature. Try placing a special birdhouse near a kitchen window, so that when you are going about the task of washing dishes or preparing food the rhythm of your efforts is accompanied by a natural song of wind and whistle.

A chime or bell hanging in a window is another way to lure the natural world into musical collaboration. These quiet melodies are so powerful at home because they inspire us to listen closely and create intimacy and peacefulness. We learn that sound can be best honored when we attune to it in a very diminished and purified state. With sound, less is more.

A PAIR OF SAND-CAST BRONZE WIND BELLS CREATE GENTLE TONES ACTIVATED BY THE WIND.

The Spirit of the Bell

The first products ever shown at Zona were bronze sandcast wind bells. Designed and crafted in Arizona by Paolo Soleri, each bell was a uniquely formed union of pattern, color, and sound. We still sell Soleri bells today, and each one is still one-of-a-kind. Here is an object whose color continues to change from the influence of weather, oxidizing in response to heat, cold, and rain. The decorative patterns of the bells, carved into the sandcast molds, are always a revelation to the touch. But the sound of each bell remains faithful to the chord it strikes when it's first rung. Since each one is completely crafted by hand, the thickness of the bell wall creates dramatic impact on the resulting tone. People choose these bells as much for their unique musical potential as for their wonderful aesthetics. The Soleri bell is our best representative of the spirit of sound, and the most revealing legacy of an artisan touched by the senses.

The best way to deal with sound inside our homes is first to identify how much amplified sound there is. Unfortunately, what rises to the forefront of our hearing is often what we would like to skim off. We are more inclined in this electronic age, however, to cover up an annoying sound by raising the volume of a pleasing one. This produces the maddening effect of creating more sound than we started with. Try peeling layers of sound away by first paying attention to the regular routine of noise you make yourself at home. Where are you the most quiet? Where does the volume of your day peak? In which rooms do layers of sound build up unabated? Creating a map of the curve of sound throughout your day will help you balance out the highs and lows and determine what base level of volume you'd like to maintain. Often this will result in a quieter, more consistently restful environment.

Music is an important subset of sound and shouldn't be taken for granted. It should be layered into the soundscape of a room last, after you have curbed the volume of all the other amplified sounds in the space. Remember as you select music for your home that recorded melody is not the only way to make music. Take into account the spoken word, live instruments, and live voices first, and save space for these sonic elements. To honor and symbolize music in your home you can put together collections of instruments, both functional and decorative, to hang on the wall or lay out casually for the impromptu performance. Even the simplest instruments have this endearing effect: Put a harmonica out on the table, and observe how often it's picked up and played, by musicians and nonmusicians alike. It is pure fun to make music.

Take care to control the quality of recorded sound you import into your space. A good sound system is a valued investment. Pay attention to where you place speakers. Note the volume on your television and phone, and lower the standard. Get a remote control for your entertainment systems with a mute button so that you can eliminate one set of sounds if you have to tune into another, like an incoming call or a conversation with your kids. Separating out and paying respect to all these different sounds in your space will help you prevent the muddied noise to which our lives so often succumb.

HOW TO | Make Music for the Home

"EVERY ROOM IN THE HOME HAS THE SOUND OF
MUSIC. SOME ROOMS ARE LOUD AND
ROCKING, OTHERS ARE SOFT AND SOOTHING. ENJOY
THE FLOW OF MUSIC IN YOUR HOME.
IN OUR OWN HOMES, WE SHOULD SEEK TO BE THE
CONDUCTORS OF THE BAND."

—LOUIS SAGAR

Music helps inform the personal perspective in a home by adding ambience and context to any event. For this reason, it's important to select the right music to go along with different activities. Making a mixed tape is a great way to tailor your musical selections to the mood of an occasion. Here are some tips on how to start the process of compiling soundtracks for your home.

First, set aside an afternoon to take stock of your favorite music. Be interdisciplinary—when you make your mix, you'll need a tape-to-tape recorder, but don't let the cassette equipment deter you from using old records or CDs. To make a mixed tape the most important tools you will require are a solid block of time and a quiet environment.

Next, think about the times you are most likely to listen to music at home, and use those moments as guidelines to set themes for a tape. Some favorites include evening meditation, brunch, or music for the harvest. If you are particularly fond of a specific type of music, say, reggae or salsa, you can also choose to create a "best-of" compilation as your theme.

Make your choices according to your theme. It's a really nice surprise to include some spoken-word selections, especially on more conceptual mixes: Try recording a passage from one of your favorite books on tape. Use the time while you are monitoring the recording of each song to relax into a magazine or book—something that doesn't require a lot of concentration, because your attention will be diverted every few minutes.

When you're done with the recording, decorate the cassette case with watercolors or cut-outs, and write out a listing of the selections on the inside cover. Remember to date your mix so that it remains a document of the time in which you made it. Music can be as potent as photography in the cataloging of important memories, so enjoy your mixed tapes over time—put them back into rotation every once in a while as a tribute to your past.

THE PLAYING OF MUSIC IN THE HOME OFTEN REVEALS ITS IMPORTANCE MANY YEARS LATER WHEN A MELODY MARKS A SPECIAL MEMORY, A CHILDHOOD FRIEND, A FAMILY GATHERING.

Scent

How often we associate the warmth of a place with the memory of a scent. Scent is nostalgia's best friend. The impression of smell lingers in us longer and evokes reflection more than any other sense. For example, the burning of piñon incense might take you back to a New Mexican adobe hearth. The sweet scent of frangipani might recall an especially fragrant walk in the Umbrian hills of Italy. We think of a scent in terms of what experiences it makes us remember, and in turn how those experiences made us feel.

This is how it works. The perception of what we smell goes directly into memory with a name: not ammonia, or lemongrass, or hickory; we smell mom's kitchen, the tropics, winter. Associations are cataloged for future reference. In this way, all the scents of the world are timeless. Once we know the smell of a charcoal barbecue, for example, made up of so many redolent components, and every time we smell barbecue afterward we'll be transported back to other memorable experiences with it. We can't describe exactly what it smells like to us. We sidestep language in our evaluation of scent. It is first a visceral, physical experience. So engaged, we can be put at ease by surrounding ourselves with a tangible collection of scents we love.

We've learned how gratifying it is to scent our living environments. One comment we hear often from people who visit Zona is how calmed they are, immediately, by the fragrance that envelops them as they walk through the door. To be sure, the first thing people perceive in any new environment, be it outdoors or indoors, is what it smells like.

At Zona, we use a combination of techniques to create our space's distinctive underpinning of scent. We burn incense first, usually something with a strong, woody undertone, like piñon or cedar. Then we apply aromatic oils in sweeter, more floral tones to small ceramic rings or discs; these are placed on heat sources, like floor lamps. The heat helps release the fragrance into the air, where it mixes with the evocative smoky tint of the incense. All invisible, but tangible to the receiving nose. Scent is encountered in a room almost like a texture.

Of course, there are other wonderful applications for scent in the home. Potpourri is site specific, and so is great to use in small areas. We'll put it out in the bathroom, by the bed, or on the console by the front door. We are big fans of whole dried elements like oranges, which hold their warm citrus perfume and are more sculptural than the shredded materials that make up most potpourris. Add a few items like these, or cinnamon sticks or dried rose heads, to your favorite potpourri blend, and you will have a mix as visually pleasing as it is redolent, worthy of display. Or, take a visual potpourri you have created out of natural materials and scent it with your favorite essential oil. One little trick we like to employ with potpourri is to display it in unexpected containers. Try placing a small amount in the mouth of a conch shell or the head of a dried sunflower. Natural element upon natural element creates a resonant still life.

Misters and atomizers are other good tools for scenting a room naturally. All that's needed is a dram or two of some essential oil and water. We are especially fond of cedar misters: The scent transports us to the forests of New Mexico, and the added moisture in the air is a good combatant against a stale or overly dry atmosphere. This is a real problem to contend with in colder months, when it's less efficient to keep windows open, despite the loss of fresh air circulation.

POTPOURRIS OF ALL KINDS START WITH SINGLE ELEMENTS FOR AN ANCHOR OF SCENT. BASIC FLORALS LIKE LAVENDER AND ROSES CAN STAND ALONE, WHILE SPICY MIXTURES FEATURING ORANGES OR CHILIS, FOR EXAMPLE, ARE STRONGLY SCENTED WITH CINNAMON.

lavender

oranges

chilis

rosebuds

You can start a new family tradition by inventing your own special scented fire.

1. Select your scenting agents. Pine needles, cedar chips, juniper berries, cinnamon sticks, orange rinds, sandalwood oil, and aromatic woods like hickory are all good bets. For an evening-long fire, you will need two to three cups of the smaller elements. Mix these materials together and set them aside.

2. Put some balled-up newspaper in the hearth—three or four pieces will do. Dab a little bit of scented oil on the sheets of paper before you ball them up.

3. Stack your kindling—smaller branches or strips of wood impregnated with fuel—around the paper so that air can move under and around each piece of wood.

4. Set one or two smaller logs on top of the kindling, and place about half of your scenting mixture in among the logs.

5. Ignite the paper throughout the kindling stack. Watch until the logs on top actually catch fire, then add a larger log. Each time you add a log, throw a bit more of your scenting mix into the hearth.

Another method of scenting and humidifying a room at the same time is to boil a small pot of water with herbs in it—things like chamomile, Greek sage, lemongrass, and mint—and let the steam waft out of the kitchen into adjoining rooms. An old Chinese tradition for sweetening the air is to lay slices of semi-dried fruits like apples and apricots on a disk atop a steamer. The same can be done in any home that has steam radiators. We also use candles, which burn in a hundred warm scents, from pure beeswax to lavender to rosemary. The heat from even the smallest flame works wonders at emanating scent.

The kitchen and bath are two significant locations for scent in the home. A lot of family nostalgia is centered around scent—the aroma of baked goods coming out of the oven, of freshly ground coffee, the fragrance of a soap we used, our mother's perfume. Displaying additional aromatics in those environments is a good way to emphasize scent in the home.

In the kitchen, you can infuse vinegars or olive oils easily. It's fun and productive to dry aromatic bundles of flowers and herbs for future use. You can even prepare your own tisane by blending some of the ingredients you've dried. Mint leaves, rosehips, and orange peel make a soothing tea. You might commit to making a savory pot of soup at the first sign of cold weather. In hot weather, with a nod to the bedroom, try sprinkling or misting pillowcases with fragrant rose water and put them in the freezer for an hour or so: Later, when they're ready to be made up on the bed for some cool relief, they'll emit a sweet floral scent.

In the bath, scent is an accepted healing agent. One of our favorite natural remedies for a cold, for example, is to rub lemon halves on the chest after a hot soak in the tub. The fruit acids seem to draw the cold right out, even as you gain perfumed citrus skin. Steaming your face with an invigorating aromatic like eucalyptus is another good way to get rid of a head cold. You can always keep a collection of scented soaps at the ready for those much-needed unwinding baths. A good way to display these is to pile them all into a big old Ball jar. That way you can delight in a tumble of beautiful packaging, and when the jar is opened to pull a bar out, an unexpected mix of fragrances emerges: vanilla, almond, jasmine, honey, sandalwood, all spun together.

Scent is highly seasonal. In the summer and spring, our sense of smell beckons us outdoors to revel in the thousand perfumes of flowers. We are equally as fond of the distinctive smell of simple clover or of the sun-warmed odor of bark and earth. To honor these scents, we follow the incentive to grow plants inside. We find that people who do their own potting have a wonderful sense of clean smells—soil, water, soap.

In the autumn and winter months, we strongly recall the smoky burn of leaves and firewood. Accordingly, a priority for many of us when we imagine our ideal home is a fireplace. The hearth is a symbol central to a family's functioning, retooled for comfort and leisure. Today we come together at the hearth, and at the first crackle of fuel set ablaze, we settle into the iconic smell of cold weather—flame on wood. And like all nostalgia of scent, we name the experience: home.

The Hand Revealed

THE SYSTEM OF OBJECTS

Objects are the last factor in the our cultivation of home, but they're our most critical source of inspiration and character. The building blocks for our material possessions should therefore be just as important as those elements we've used to embellish the aesthetics or heighten the sensory profiles of our homes.

Wood, fiber, glass, stone, metal, clay: Forged, molded, woven, and carved into commodious shape by human hands, these raw materials marry form to function in the everyday objects that populate our homes. We import these materials into our space in the shape of furnishings because they offer up a more sensual experience than industrial objects would. This is why we search for the right antique wooden desk instead of using an institutional Formica model in our home office, and why we invest in ceramic mixing bowls and wooden cutting boards for our kitchen instead of plastic ones. At Zona, we look for objects transformed out of the most beautiful materials.

AN ARTISAN'S HAND REVEALS THE SPLENDOR OF A SCULPTED STONE EGG FROM THE PRIMITIVE ISLAND OF KALIMANTAN. THE SYMBOLS OF TIME INSCRIBED ON THE EXTERIOR ARE BELIEVED TO BRING A YEAR OF GOOD LUCK.

Bamboo

"THE CRAFTS OF BAMBOO ARE VERY PURE.
THIS IS BECAUSE BAMBOO ITSELF AS A RAW MATERIAL
HAS ALMOST NO FINANCIAL VALUE.
THUS THE ESTIMATION SET ON THOSE ARTICLES MADE
BY MASTERS DERIVES ENTIRELY FROM THE
SKILL AND ART OF THEIR HANDS. IT IS THE CRAFTS-
MANSHIP ITSELF WHICH IS PRIZED."

—KOICHIRO UEDA

They call it "take" in Japan, in China "chu." Here in the West we call it bamboo. In Asia, bamboo is considered one of the four noble plants—the others being the orchid, plum blossoms, and the chrysanthemum. Bamboo grows faster than any other living botanical. This plant—it is not a tree—reaches its full size in the first two months of life and remains at its adult height for a hundred years or more. At the minimum, there remain more than fifteen hundred surviving species of bamboo in the world. Its abundance is a gift to all the ecological and cultural systems that rely on it.

Flexible, durable, and amazingly lightweight for its strength, the artisan elevates bamboo, as a raw material, to the stature of royalty. Bamboo weds the most basic functional needs with elegant aesthetics. Entire shelters can be constructed out of it, as well as the smallest of tools and utensils. Bamboo is also a food source and is widely known for its medicinal properties. Indeed, to walk in a bamboo grove is to experience a true and healing communion with nature. The power of this pristine material authenticates the need to connect our lives and our homes to the textural and elemental. Find a space in your home for an artisan object made from bamboo. It may just become one of your most favored treasures.

A GROVE OF BAMBOO STALKS DEMONSTRATES THE POWER
OF ITS FORM, COLOR, AND PATTERN.

Raw Materials

FIBER

Fiber for Zona is silk, cotton, wool, and linen. Fabric is felt, canvas, flannel, velvet, muslin, and chenille. We use fiber throughout our homes in ways large and small: for our table, certainly for the bed, and especially for upholstery. Upholstered furniture makes a room comfortable and adds an immediate sense of welcome. We always like to include some sort of easy chair or sofa, or at least cushion, in every room, including the kitchen.

Textiles afford a room an extra aspect of luxury and texture. You can dress almost every surface area, including the walls and floors, with interchangeable fiber elements—throws, pillows, blankets, placemats, carpets, decorative hangings. This is our favorite way to alter the atmosphere of a room and bears little of the expense and effort involved in painting or replacing furniture. Using textiles also allows us to explore and layer pattern in a space. A beautiful silk embroidered pillow or vintage lace tablecloth, for example, elevates the larger, more abstract form dressed underneath.

Sensitive care for your fabric possessions ensures their long life. Good agents to include in the hand-laundering of delicate textiles are a dousing of white vinegar or salt and a little bit of clarified rose or orange water. Instead of storing unused textiles in closed containers or cabinets, display them on shelves or in open trunks. The circulation of air through the woven material will stabilize all but the most fragile heirloom fabrics. If storage is a necessity, wrap each piece in a few leaves of ink-free tissue paper and throw in a handful of lavender before storing. This element is a wonderful and fragrant alternative to preservatives like cedar or camphor.

WOOD

A home doesn't feel quite anchored without the inclusion of some wood elements, either as furnishings or as architectural detail. For example, a hardwood floor is a wonderful feature to play up in the absence of any major wood furniture pieces. We especially like to see furniture

made out of pine, cypress, and walnut, all of which have subtle grains and natural, rustic tones. Our favorite wooden pieces include tables of all sizes, chairs, cupboards and wardrobes, and shelving.

Wood also has the wonderful property of being very paintable. We love to mix the intense color and texture of antique painted wood pieces, like chests and stepback cupboards, with more subdued contemporary furnishings. Wood is a great material to search for in the antiques market because it does age and patina so beautifully. When you are collecting vintage pieces made of iron or stone, you are far less likely to get the same character from the material itself.

A fine way to determine old or highly crafted wood furniture is to look at the joinings. Hand-forged square nails are good signs of age and quality, as are wide boards and tendon joints without any nails or glue at all. Staples are frequently a sign of economy in construction, and should be watched for.

GLASS

Glass is a wonderful and precious accent material. It is by tradition smooth and clear and utilitarian, but we've found all sorts of decorative glass objects in recent years that are highly tactile and unusually colorful. We are always searching for interesting vases and serving pieces, too, which mix glass with a complementary material like gold or silver leaf or pewter. Glass lampshades spun in jewel tones or set Tiffany-style in close harmony with shells, deliver immediate elegance to the most functional reading light. We tend to keep glass items on the small side at home and let the impact of what they hold—flowers, food, natural elements, or simply light—draw in the eye.

Antique glass is a wonderful collectible because it's so plentiful and still affordable. One of the best ways to identify an old piece of glass is to look for cutting marks where the item was severed from the blowing tube. Glass plates and bottles that look like they have seams are cast rather than blown, and won't be as old as other examples. Look also for inconsistencies in thickness and texture: These are good signs that a piece has been hand-blown.

STONE

Since stone is a heavy, massive material, we tend to use it for large items like tables and counters. Stone provides an excellent counterpoint to other opaque materials like wood and iron. We often employ these elements in combination: For example, we'll use a chestnut base for a stone tabletop or cut stone shelves to fit into an airily constructed etagere. Stone mantelpieces are wonderful to highlight, or even install, if a hearth space boasts a beautiful wood floor. We like to keep stone in as natural a state as possible, so we favor matte finishes, granites, and slate over polished onyx or marble.

Small-scale stone works well with clay and water to create a garden feeling inside. You can use natural rocks and pebbles to add texture and completeness to potted plants or bulbs. One of our favorite examples is the naturally smooth Japanese river rock. When stone is dampened, whether in an indoor fountain, a decorative birdbath, or just in a bowl full of pebbles and water, we re-create the evocative feel of a riverbed or beach, and draw the natural world deeper into our interiors.

We love the fluid, linear aspect of metal, and we import it into all manner of decorative home furnishings.

The strength and solid presence of metal is well used to offset delicate elements. A beautiful hand-wrought chandelier suspending light or a tall standing candlestick bearing a fragile honeycombed votive are great examples of a heavy element used to bear a light one. We see the same thing with pewter or silver stems supporting fine glasswork. Because metal is almost always a neutral color, we can give ourselves over to the visual tricks it plays with its weight and sheen, if it's polished or gilded.

We encourage the natural oxidation of metal throughout many of the architectural details in a home. This creates patina, as with wood, and patina creates character. Try, for example, letting brass sink fixtures or wall sconces oxidize. Because of the diversity in the surface properties of the material, metal is one of the few elements that looks well in groupings with other metals. A green-toned bronze pitcher fits in well with a silver serving piece or polished pair of candlesticks. A hand-forged iron bowl filled with paper clips meshes nicely with a pewter letter opener and magnifying glass on an old-fashioned desk blotter.

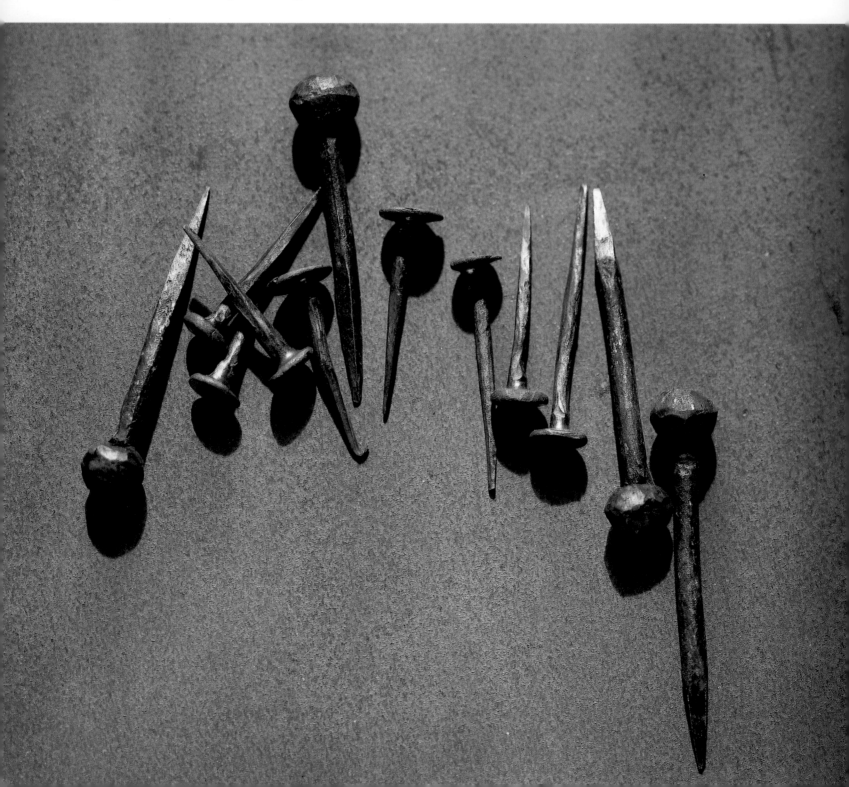

Clay is the most elemental material, and perhaps the easiest to understand. We can all envision putting our hands around a lump of clay and shaping it into a vessel of sorts. There is no end of containers we will collect to make the most of this material: pitchers, bowls, vases, plates, and mugs.

We look for ceramic containers that exploit color and texture. Pigments and glazes can be applied to an artful level on clay, creating one-of-a-kind pieces out of the most utilitarian forms. Vintage Mexican ceramics are a wonderful model of this aesthetic, as are pieces from Eastern Europe, if you can find them.

Presenting clay in an atypical context usually means employing it in a large item or over a large surface area. A ceramic tabletop is one marvelous recasting of this intimate material. Our exceptional and favorite example of this work comes in the form of huge tabletops made in Italy. Ceramic tiles can serve as a great earthy counterpoint to other structural materials in the home, especially in the kitchen and bath. Beautifully painted tiles can be used as decorations for a wall.

The Craft of Hands

The creative hand is what ties together all of the natural materials we bring into our homes and what makes the resulting objects so special to us. We elevate the significance of the hand in our homes by living with hand-made things. The echo of fingers on a hand-woven shawl or the irregular pattern left by a hammer on a copper pot gives us a sense of union with the greater world from which these materials come. We somehow feel more balanced, for example, if our kitchen, replete with gadgetry of all kinds, is integrated with simple additions like a hand-made cutting board of bird's-eye maple and a set of earthenware dishes.

Our approach to the hand-made has always been to look to past traditions of craft, updated for contemporary use. This has given us the opportunity to develop not only a collective of exceptional, highly styled objects for the home, but also a family of skilled artists working in traditions we need to support. Craftspeople are becoming an endangered species as machines and industry and neglect of tradition wither the demand for functional items made of natural materials. We feel that we're in danger of losing much more than the knowledge base for simple decorative craft as we hurtle toward the future; we also lose the native, familial wisdom that goes along with essential objects like a clay pitcher for wine or a carved hardwood mixing spoon.

At Zona, the narrative of the hand that made a piece is told through the contour of a well-carved silhouette or the sharp precision of a beveled edge. We perceive quality in such details, and accordingly bestow more faith in the objects that carry them. As a result, we really find that we use those objects more and lessen our need for duplicates. We become better conservationists in our own homes. And supported by that knowledge, we can start eliminating the clutter and accumulation that diminishes our sense of comfort. We now know how to elevate spatial elements, homemade sensory remedies, and hand-made objects of beauty, to build a meaningful, personal atmosphere. We have taken all the tools in hand, and we are ready to embrace the craft of creating home for ourselves.

Christine Salusti

THE CERAMACIST

Texture is all important in the work of ceramist Christine Salusti. In her studio, vessels of clay become otherworldly forms: Surfaces may at first be perceived through glaze and gilding, but their impact comes most from touch. There is mystery in the contrast between the perfectly smooth, black interiors of her pieces and the roughly patterned fossil and shell pressings she uses on the exterior. Called "spirit" bowls for the precious items they're meant to hold, Salusti's works use texture as a metaphor for her own sense of the outer and the inner: "I'm always involved with contrasts of different textures, smooth and rough. I like the conflict between something very primitive and something very elegant." Christine Salusti came to ceramics by way of stone carving. She views the solo interplay of hand on clay as a fitting homage to her years spent as a sculptor in New York City. Working with one's hands, she says, is a universal art form.

Michèlle Ratté

THE PRINTMAKER

A veteran printmaker and studio artist, Michèlle Ratté discovered fiber as a medium by accident. Ratté does not weave fabric; she reconstructs it, yard by yard, until her beautiful silks, velvets, and linens emerge as objects bearing a new imprint. Today, the hand-tooling she uses to craft her fabrics has become integral to her sense of art-making: "I draw a lot of strength and power from the environment—the sea, the beach. It's an interesting thing to contemplate where your inspiration comes from." A resident of Martha's Vineyard, Ratté consistently draws from nature to develop the iconic motifs and rich colorings that are central to her work. She strives for intricate detail in her printing techniques to complement the beauty of the raw textile: In each piece that leaves her workshop, the visual and the textural are woven together like warp and weft.

Leigh Morrell

THE BLACKSMITH

Leigh Morrell has been around iron all his life. He grew up on a Morgan horse farm in Vermont and started shoeing horses for a living when he was twenty. He moved to ornamental smithing some years later, to safeguard both his weakened back and his personal creativity. Anchoring his production with ancient forge-welding techniques, his shop has been busy ever since: **"I don't produce art that doesn't have a function. You can embellish a simple item and make it very pretty; but, from my perspective, if you have a utilitarian object, make it do its job first. When I look at a piece, I want to see clean lines."** He seeks to reinterpret traditional items—tall standing candlesticks, fireplace tools and screens—with Old World skill and contemporary acumen. The resulting ironworks are what he likes to think of as new heirlooms, sturdy enough to last yet another generation.

Robert Sonday

THE WOODWORKER

Robert Sonday began building chairs because he saw that people needed comfortable places to sit. Influenced not only by a Shaker purity of form but also by an intentional use of color to clarify line, he began using the exotic hued woods that are today his trademark: "I'm very mechanical. I like machines. I have this passion for equipment, and I have a passion for furniture with a real fine line to it. I can bring those two passions together with my chairs." Robert Sonday makes thirty-one different types of seating, all from the same single components. He produces his furniture the old-fashioned way: on his own, at his lathe, turning individual parts one at a time and piecing them together. His workshop is also the back of his home, an old renovated country store in Virginia. He laughs at the proprietary use of his living space as a showroom, but admits that it's a great proving ground: If a chair isn't proportioned right, or isn't comfortable enough to sit in, it won't last long in his household or his line.

Dian Needham

THE FURNITURE MAKER

Even as a little girl growing up in New Jersey Dian Needham knew she wanted to make furniture. What is wondrous is that this diminutive woman came to conquer the sleek urban furniture mecca of New York City with her own brand of rustic farmwood furniture and shelving: "From my earliest memories I was always trying to build something, always creating, but with my hands. I think I chose wood because I am the type of designer who designs with a function in mind. Furniture is the best way to create something that you have to use." Working out of a former stable in Manhattan's Lower East Side with one assistant, Needham creates the aura of a more natural life with her simple utilitarian furniture. Needham uses her own home as a research center in order to uncover what basics she should be building next: barnwood medicine cabinets for the bathroom; tiered shelving systems for places where a whole bookcase won't fit; large vintage-stained frames for mirrors; media units with charming shuttered fronts for unsightly electronics. This modern furniture maker utilizes a rough-hewn style in the selection of woods and finishes to help restore a respect for both function and form.

In the Element of Air

Winter

air is sky and weather. Clouds dance in formation to make an ocean above our heads; wind is a messenger of scent and sound. Air truly feels itself, though, in the absence of these things. It is the most forceful element in the desert, the magnificent mediator of open space from a rugged mesa to a parched lowland plain.

"THE ARTISANS OF THE AMERICAN
SOUTHWEST ARE CARETAKERS FOR THE LAND, AND
THEIR WORKS DEPICT THE ORIGINS
AND ROOTS OF THEIR CULTURE AND HERITAGE."

—Louis Sagar

New Mexico

In America, there is a rarefied air to the desert skies of the Southwest. In the heat and stillness, the air has preserved civilizations far older than our own. The spirit of the artisan has in this way crystallized in Native American cultures throughout the region.

The Navajo, Zuni, and Hopi peoples are just a few of the caretakers on this land. Air and sky are blue here, abundantly rendered in turquoise and set in silver. Weavings, pottery, and baskets are decorated with symbolic motifs that recount the tales of elemental gods. The spiritual aesthetic that pervades even everyday objects is well conserved and elegantly captured in the decorative crafts of these ancient cultures. When I place a small Apache basket or a black pot from Santa Clara in my home, I breathe the crisp dry air of the pueblo. Air is encouraged to move at will around the well-contoured form of a vessel or through the wide geometry of a rug. The objects themselves invite the element into collaboration, to conjure up rain and wind and snow, and carry the spirit of traditions past into the ever-dependent present.

3

Creating the Space

What Is

The making of a home is about telling a story. Each story is unique. In my home, I render the story of my life. In your home, you render the story of your life. Each one of our home-making activities has a role to play to help enact the story. The daily cleaning and polishing of our homes—the arranging of flowers, the painting of a room, the preparations we do for the holidays: these are all elements of the tale. Home decorating is the art of telling it well. ¶ Decorating is also about expressing a distinctive interior style. After prioritizing for comfort and surrounding ourselves with objects of meaning and beauty, the term "style" becomes the symbolic hybrid of all a home's different identities. Style evolves into an internal code by which you determine the look and functionality of each aspect of your aesthetic. Selecting a few key design words to represent the various elements of that aesthetic can be very helpful when creating an overall decorating plan. ¶ I call Zona's style a blend of the rustic and the elegant. The earthy texture of a carved New Mexican Sabino table mixes well with a pair of Florentine iron candleholders, hand-rubbed with aged gold leaf. Rustic elegance integrates the modern, the ancient, and the timeless feel of the countryside. Matte finishes and natural paints in vegetable colors are representative of the style. I love to use natural fabrics—I favor linen, wool, and organic cotton. Rattan, raffia, and bamboo are plant materials that are ideal for application in rustic furnishings and construction; hand-painted terra-cotta tiles from countries such as Morocco, Mexico, and Turkey are elegant as accents in kitchens and in bath areas. All these materials typify for me a feel that goes along with my touchstone style. ❡ The artistry of different cultures contributes to and enhances my style at home. I am often inspired by ethnic elements and antique artifacts. Objects are especially appealing to me when their surfaces and finishes become worn with the patina of age. In keeping with this sensibility, the concepts of weathered and washed finishes for natural wood furnishings were pioneered at Zona. With design conventions like these ornamenting the concept of the natural home, my style has become anchored and viable. ❡ When you begin decorating, it's best to choose a framework like this to work with—one that transcends period distinctions and expresses a classic style for the home over the long term. Rustic elegance has been borne out in many different furnishings and room settings over the years; yet the style is still flexible enough to represent Zona's evolving sensibility.

Decorating?

Maintaining Focus

Your home's mission statement will be a very helpful tool when establishing your interior style. Decorating projects should feed into the overall goals of your home, whether they're small activities you can do over a weekend or long-term design adjustments that require professional support. Stay clear on the following key points when embarking on any home decorating venture, and especially when seeking outside consultation:

1. CLARITY OF VISION FOR THE LONG-TERM GOALS

2. CLEAR DEFINITION OF CURRENT FUNCTIONAL NEEDS

3. BUDGETARY FRAME OF REFERENCE

4. COMMITMENT TO STAYING INVOLVED FROM THE START THROUGH TO THE FINISH

The careful placement of furnishings and objects in my home creates a bond with the things I own. I like the idea of everything having its own spot, however transitory that spot may be. When I present my possessions I assess the spatial characteristics of the area I'm putting them in. I want them placed at the right height. I want the space around them to be distinct. Thoughtful context and harmonious proportions allow my furnishings to be noticed and appreciated. Large and receptive surfaces, like tables and shelves, are ideal for object placement and display. Arriving at a satisfactory display comprises big moves and small moves. It takes time. Dedicate enough time to the practice of object placement in your own home, and you will come to know how wonderfully flexible your interior space can be.

AN EXAMPLE OF A LIVING ROOM IN WHICH THE WALL ELEMENTS ARE PLACED TO ACHIEVE A BALANCE AND HARMONY WITH THE OBJECTS SET BEHIND THE SOFA AND THE COLORFULLY PATTERNED PILLOWS ARRANGED IN FRONT.

Placement of Objects:
Three Points to Remember

1. BALANCE AND HARMONY OF MATERIALS

Determine the ideal placement for an object by first placing it on a table by itself. Proportions and details are easier to identify this way. Effective placement requires a sensitivity to material. For example, glass and metal always look and sound good when placed on a wood surface. Wood objects look beautiful on stone. Conversely, a metal candleholder placed on a glass table can sound harsh and feel cold. Offset difficulties like this with fiber, linen, straw, and cork—all excellent intermediaries to bring objects of diverse material into balance. Textiles and fiber can, in general, weave harmony between contrasting masses and textures. Use them as well to soften spaces that feel hard and to warm up surfaces that seem cold. Clay is universal. It can work beautifully as a complement to glass, stone, and wood. Clay on metal surfaces, however, can be a difficult combination.

2. COLORS COMPLEMENT OTHER COLORS

I love objects of primary color to be placed on dry natural surfaces. Objects of neutral or natural color present themselves well when placed on furnishings of similar color. Color also works well in themes: everything in shades of blue, everything in shades of red. Clean pale backdrop colors—light yellows, blues, and whites—are better than neutral earthy tones for keeping objects of bright color looking vivid.

3. CONTEXT AND DISCOVERY

Experiment with placing objects in a context that is unexpected. Reveal the personality of a favorite object by highlighting it under a focused light. Place common objects in a grouping of three or five—odd numbers are best when grouping objects. Repeat a pleasing form, like a candlestick or a pitcher, in all its variations, to create a series.

Essentials

Essentials are the classics of your home. We know most people collect beloved things over the course of many years as their sensibilities and budgets permit, so these pieces represent broad housekeeping function with flexible aesthetics. We love these items simply because they make us feel at home, no matter how they're painted, carved, or cast.

A **SMALL STOOL**, old and saturated with layers of paint, or carved out of a fine wood, or cast in metal and polished bright, for the pedestaled display of art and artifacts

A **TRUNK**, of boned canvas or leather, or carved in Sabino wood and set on its own stand, or painted a bright blue, green, or yellow, for visual impact and storage and additional tabletop space

A **KID'S CHEST**, constructed of cardboard or painted wood, or made of shiny metal, for safe and accessible storage of toys and games

A **COFFEE TABLE**, carved of ponderosa pine or made of old wide boards, or a simple stone or glass tabletop on a special base, or painted with a pattern many years ago and left to fade, for showing collections and books in an accessible way, and to serve as a comfortable spot for informal dining

A **ROCKER**, cast in metal and stripped of paint, or ancient and creaking in old wood, or expertly crafted with a hand-woven seat, for the peaceful rhythm that it brings to intimate moments of relaxation

CONTAINERS for flowers, large and small, ceramic pitchers and tall glass vases, vintage milk bottles and hammered copper urns, silver bowls and drilled stones, all for the presentation of beautifully colored and scented blooms

CANDLEHOLDERS, forged of iron or cast in pewter, carved of cherry wood, gleaming in glass or brass or bronze, diminutive and tall alike, for the display of a home's most atmospheric and soothing light

A **PRECIOUS BOX**, wrapped in raffia or fine rice paper, formed of leather, hammered in silver, or reclaimed and polished of old wood, with many drawers or none at all, for the keeping of sacred private mementos

A **WELCOME MAT**, woven of jute or straw or twigs, or hand-hooked and backed in canvas, to greet guests and family alike with warmth and hospitality

A **MIRROR**, of old glass with engraved flowers or framed by wood, carved or gilt, set into an old window pane, or mounted as an art piece in conjunction with photography, to reflect spirit and energy through our space

A **CLOCK**, set in pewter, or sporting vintage style, made of found objects or hand-painted components, for the wall or desk, to tell the time with grace and beauty

A **LAMP** of ambient beauty, with a wooden or iron or bronze base, shaded in jewel tones of stained or swirled glass, hushed by parchment or mica or linen, to create private corners of light in larger spaces, for intimate occupation

A **CHIME OR BELL**, of cast bronze and molded clay, in copper or hand-made with metal fragments, to bring spontaneous music into our homes

A **BREADBOARD**, carved in a contoured rectangle or a circle, in bird's-eye maple, cherry, or marble, for the ritual of breaking bread

A SET OF BOWLS, nesting inside each other or diversely collected over time, hand-painted or utility white, ceramic or wood or glass, to grace the preparing and serving of food

TOASTING GLASSES, hand-blown and selected for individual beauty, forged in silver, or stemmed with pewter, to encourage a gathering of praise and thanks around all the special events of a home

A MUG, for each member of the family, hand-shaped in clay, painted and patterned, or wide-brimming in vintage enamel, or heat pressurized in colorful glass, to promote the savoring of warm, aromatic drinks every day

AN AREA RUG OR CARPET, woven geometrically in jute or linen, or precious in hue and pattern from a kilim weave, or bright and smooth in luxurious cut pile, for the lovely anchor and texture it provides our underappreciated floors

A PAIR OF BOOKENDS, cast in fantastic shapes of iron or made of thick glass, reinterpreted as an old or bronzed pair of boots, or a pair of heavy vintage trophies, to preserve and make accessible our essential books

A GATHERING BASKET, woven in broad strips or tightly braided coils, tray-shaped or deep and elaborately handled, made of rustic twigs or covered in birch bark, to provide gracious transport and staging for our favorite cuttings and garden vegetables

STATIONERY, heavy cotton or sheer parchment, embedded with flowers or primed by a watermark, brightly colored or vanilla-white, formally monogrammed or simple and utilitarian, boxed with matching envelopes or delightfully mismatched, to encourage the memorable power of communication in the hand-written word

DISPLAY STANDS OR EASELS, simply constructed of iron or elaborately carved from wood, sculpturally formed of glass or clay brick, or a fragment of slate, to highlight and anchor delicate objects of beauty

SHELVING FOR PRESENTATION, free-standing, built-in, or incorporated as a visual unit into a piece of furniture, thickly transparent in glass, heavy in wood and stone and tile, highly neutral in color and texture, to harbor collections, books, and still lifes in linear, serial space

A WORK TABLE OR DESK, reinvented for comfort and beauty from elegant materials—glass, stone, wood—or imported in as an old workbench, or oversized for a display of extra equipment and objects, to centralize and honor the tools of intellectual labor

PICTURE FRAMES, cast in precious metals, wrapped in dried elements like tobacco leaves, preciously fragile in leaded and mosaic glass, rustic in barnwood, modern in metal, and always abundant, to memorialize images of beauty and document portraits of family all around the home. Small sterling frames are ideal for bedroom vanities, inlaid wood and antique frames for fireplace mantels and desks.

Buy Furniture for Your Home

Family legacies aside, we all have the need at one time or another to buy furniture. Whether you're looking for antique or newly crafted furniture to fill out the landscape of your home, any major pieces you invest in (always starting with those on your own essentials list) are destined to become heirlooms. What are the important considerations to have in mind before actually making a purchase? How can you be sure to meet your criteria of quality and longevity? Here is a checklist to help you make successful and meaningful furniture purchases.

DINING ROOM TABLES

Make an objective evaluation of where you spend the most time eating. There are normally two choices: in the kitchen or in the dining room. Some families require both. Open plans with one large table, demonstrated so well in loft living, are also an option. Kitchens allow for informality and activity; dining rooms are often formal and underutilized.

Know in advance how many people you ideally need to accommodate, and how often you'll be seating large parties. Narrow your choice of materials. I always recommend wood, but stone and glass can also work. Shape is very important. Round or rectangular tables are preferable. Know your minimum and maximum size requirements, as

they relate to the proportions of your space. My favorite size in a round is 54 inches, which will accommodate four people. You can accommodate eight people at an 84- by 42-inch rectangle. Never buy a dining table more than 31 inches high; 29 to 30 inches is an ideal height, one that most chairs will work with. Do your best to acquire the maximum size for your needs. Always leave room for the placement of foods and flowers as centerpieces. Make sure to ask about the durability of the materials, and check that maintenance will not be problematic. If you have kids, ensure that corners are rounded. Last but not least, absolutely double-check that your table will fit not just in the space, but through the front door and up any stairs.

DINING ROOM CHAIRS

I consider table chairs the most difficult purchase of all. A well-constructed, comfortable chair can cost a great deal. Chairs that are not well built will not last. The method of construction is critical. Emphasize comfort over design, although you can achieve both.

When shopping for a chair, always do three things. Sit in the chair. Lean back in the chair, recline deeply. Feel the chair's range of comfort. I like chairs that have some pitch to the back support and are not too rigid. You should also

turn the chair over and inspect how it is constructed: If you are not sufficiently knowledgeable to judge, a good salesperson will be quick to educate you. The fewer nails you see, the better. Leg joinery to the seat should be well and artfully reinforced. Ideal seat depth is 16 inches and 18 inches is a good sitting height.

Chairs should not be too heavy visually. Try folding chairs in tight spaces. I find a cushioned seat can soften an angular frame shape. Tie-on cushions can be added to wooden chairs with unforgiving seats. I prefer sets of old chairs with new tables, although chairs in a set do not have to be all in the same style. This type of mismatching makes antique options more viable, since it's very rare and often prohibitively expensive to collect complete old sets. Modern wooden chairs with Shaker-style woven fabric seating are versatile and classic.

BEDS

The mattress is the key. Make the investment here first. Keep proportions of bed selections in balance with the size of your room. The choice of frame design should integrate into your overall interior theme. Antique beds can be romantic and very visually appealing, but make sure of sizing for linens and sheets. I like beds that sit low to the floor. A high quality futon on a low frame can provide this intimate scale. Refrain from overemphasizing the masculine or feminine in your bed dressing. Always pay careful attention to your bed's orientation to incoming light.

UPHOLSTERED SEATING

Upholstered seating will provide the primary silhouette within the space of a living or family room. Approach the customizing of upholstered sofas and chairs in the same manner that you would approach the purchase of a suit. First, the piece or pieces must be fitted to the space. Then consider the fabric, the styling, the tailoring, and the internal construction. The combination of frame scale, fabric selection, and styling (type of design) determine the look of the sofa. The scale of the piece will help you determine the aura of the surrounding space: intimate or vast. Fabric often represents a substantial part of the cost of the seating. Make an investment here to guarantee the durability and long-term attractiveness of your chosen material. Natural fibers will always wear best, in terms of fabric strength, patina, and textural hand.

When you sit in a sofa or chair make sure that your feet

can reach the ground comfortably. Place both hands on the arms. Try and stick to a firm seat, but never invest in an overly stiff cushion: Breakdown of shape can be uneven and there will be insufficient physical give. You will know that you are in the right upholstered chair when you feel the fabric and form gently flexing to accommodate you.

A CHEST OF DRAWERS

Chests of drawers are purchased to provide storage. It is wise to invest in an all-purpose chest with simple, flexible aesthetics. Smooth drawer movement is a test of quality, and drawer pulls should be easy to the touch. Depth of the drawers is the central consideration—stay away from chests that have too many thin drawers. Drawers that are too deep (more than 6 inches) can lead to cluttered storage. Look for pieces of unusual height that can provide visual sweep and help balance out the mass of other large pieces in a room, like a bed or desk.

OPPOSITE: THIS VINTAGE BED SET IN A CONNECTICUT HOME HAS A VISUALLY STRIKING HEADBOARD THAT ESTABLISHES A CENTER POINT FOR THE ENTIRE ROOM. NOTICE THE LOVELY PATINA OF THE ORIGINAL GREEN PAINT.

Heirlooms

When we become more selective in the essentials we purchase for our homes, we create the opportunity for more of them to become heirlooms in the future. We are attentive to the choice of material, the quality of design, and method of craftsmanship. We are thoughtful about how our furnishings will meet our functional needs. We practice the art of learning to see: Our interior aesthetic is activated, placement has been considered, and we begin at last to deeply enjoy the decorative appeal of the furnishings we choose to live with.

Heirlooms are not defined by what is old or new: Heirlooms are timeless. They are both the smallest sacred things and the most important investment pieces in your home. The seasons come and go, the years pass, but an heirloom holds shape, retains character, and develops patina. You can tell that there's a story behind any heirloom piece, right away. These items are never neutral.

Heirlooms have what I call sensorial resonance. They capture our hearts and transcend their original function. Look at a rocking chair, for example. Expectant mothers love their rocking chairs for resting. Young babies are soothed by the rhythmic movement. Children climb onto the laps of their fathers to hear bedtime stories. Grandfathers reminisce before taking a nap. The rocking chair receives; it stretches; it deepens its status in the order of the home. It becomes a symbol as much as a place of comfort for anyone who cares to sit.

Personal belongings can also become heirlooms. I have a travel guide to Thailand filled with notes, articles, and penciled-in tips. It holds cards from restaurants that served memorable meals. It is partly a diary, partly a commentary on the guide itself. I keep it as an heirloom not only for its marvelous graphic narrative, but also for the experience of nostalgia it calls up in me whenever I handle it. My old baseball caps, my handmade beads, letters I wrote as a youngster in summer camp, a pair of paint-stained khakis: These are all heirlooms, to be displayed inventively and proudly. We honor such items by raising them up out of retirement and seeing them anew, as artifacts of aesthetic as much as nostalgic value.

HOW TO | Hang a Picture

I have always considered framed photographs, drawings, and paintings to be of primary importance in decorating. A piece of art can serve as a point of reference in determining the color palette of a room. The purchase of both art and frame should be undertaken with the same care you attach to your furniture investments.

Here are some practical tips on how to incorporate art into your space cohesively and securely.

1. **NEVER BE IN A RUSH** to cover up your walls with artwork. There is nothing wrong with a wall that is bare and waiting for the right acquisition.

2. **WALLS GIVE US AN OPPORTUNITY TO BE INVENTIVE** and unconventional with dimensional materials. Take this opportunity to frame an object out of context. The framing of a personal heirloom or of a collection of common objects—like pencils, old playing cards, or natural dried elements—can be inexpensive and lots of fun.

3. **AS AN ALTERNATIVE TO FRAMED ART, CREATE A WALL SETTING OUT OF INDEPENDENT TEXTURAL ELEMENTS.** Buy a number of forged-iron hooks and fix them to the walls as if they were a peg rack. Hang a collection of baskets or sculptural forms like old bowed saws in a row. Or display textiles from your closet: silk scarves, colorful summer sarongs, a collection of lap blankets. Walls act as storage: In private spaces, use hooks to display strands of beads and jewelry.

4. **ALWAYS LAY OUT ON THE FLOOR WHAT YOU INTEND TO PLACE ON THE WALL.** Experiment with your arrangement before putting nails in the wall.

5. **FRAMES ARE ALWAYS WORTH THE INVESTMENT.** Large frames create dimension and scale; small frames encourage focus. I prefer frames that create borders and establish a territory for the work presented. Wood is my material of choice. Antique gold and aged platinum are my favorite finishes for frames, but colorful paint can be amusing and festive. Natural wood tones are safe, and black is consistent. Vintage frames can be affordable and add distinct character. Try hanging a collection of beautiful frames without any works inside for a sculptural still life on your wall or select an especially graceful frame for a simple mirror.

A Word on Family Photographs

There is nothing more precious to the home than family photographs. These are essential heirlooms in the making. How often we neglect to have our favorite photographs, of the children or our parents, properly framed! After the initial excitement, and a few looks here or there, the prints sit in their envelopes in a drawer.

Whenever you develop photographs, do your best to make two sets. Keep one set complete for an album and choose images to frame from the other. From a thirty-six-print roll, you are doing well if three or four photographs deserve the posterity of framing. You need not rush off to buy frames right away. Place those few photos you intend to frame on a shelf or table near your bedside. Enjoy the photos. Obtain a letter box or container to store these special images. Begin your search for the appropriate frames. Visit your favorite shops and antique shows. Hunt some down at flea markets.

Ask your older relatives to send you some old unframed family photographs. Dedicate a year in which the primary gifts you give are framed family photos. Date each one with both the year the picture was taken and the year it was given. Over time, create your own special collection and hang the pictures on a favorite wall. Add to the gallery of images when you take or discover new photos of quality and cultivate a visual family tree.

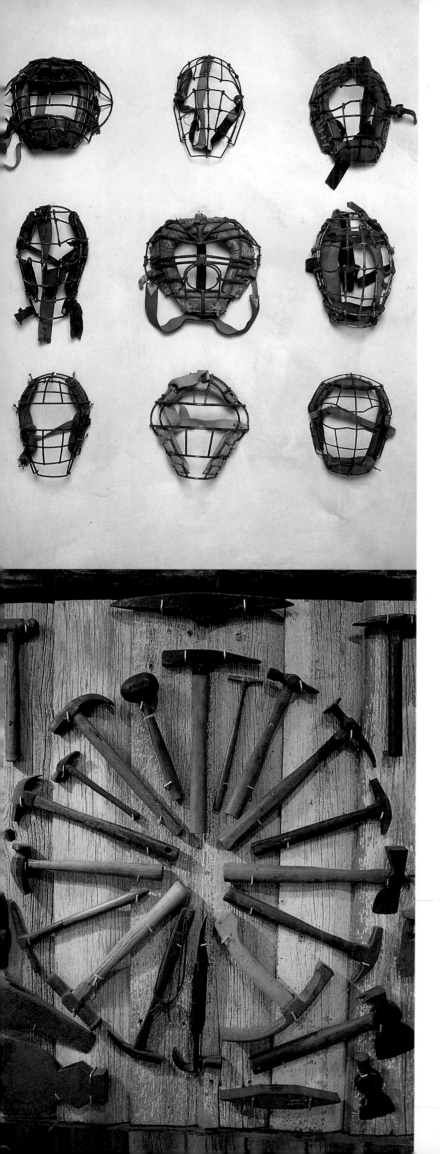

Collections

"THERE ARE NEW COLLECTIBLES BEING
INVENTED EVERY MOMENT. THE MOST COMMON ELE-
MENTS, ONES WHICH WE TEND TO TAKE FOR
GRANTED IN EVERYDAY LIFE ARE OFTEN THE SOURCES
OF OUR MOST BEAUTIFUL COLLECTIONS."

—LOUIS SAGAR

The display of collections often contributes wonderfully to the aesthetics of a home. We all develop great pride in our collections: They become archival and each component has a history. Objects gathered to form a collection invariably stimulate curiosity on the part of the visitor; they become part of the introduction to a space's inhabitants.

The past, the present, and the future all have distinct roles in the development of a grouping. Older objects have a context from their own history—where they come from, what they were used for. Newly made collected objects may have a unique cultural value, but will require the test of time to prove their resonance. How surprised and respectful we are when we see a collectible in mint condition. Start your collections by first taking a look around. There are new collectibles being invented every moment. The individual choices we make help reinforce our personal sense of style, and provide us with the tremendous fun of hunting down and gathering up new additions at regular intervals.

FROM A COLLECTION OF NINE VINTAGE CATCHERS MASKS TO A VARIETY SCISSORS OR CARPENTRY HAMMERS, THE ATTENTION TO DETAIL IN PLACEMENT AND PRESENTATION IS WHAT MAKES THESE GROUPINGS COME ALIVE. NOTICE THE SUCCESSFUL REPETITION OF THESE OBJECTS IN SIMPLE GEOMETRIC GRIDS, PATTERNED ON SQUARES AND CIRCLES.

HOW TO | Build Ideas for Collections

> "A COLLECTION IS THE SUM OF A SERIES OF DECISIONS,
> CHANCES, ACCIDENTS, QUIRKS, AND OTHER INSTANCES OF HAPPENSTANCE.
> YOU FIND A BAD PIECE HERE, YOU LOSE A GOOD ONE THERE, YOU PAY
> TOO MUCH HERE, YOU GET A STEAL THERE. THAT'S THE ORGANIC QUALITY
> OF A COLLECTION AND YOU LIVE IN IT—YOU INHABIT
> ITS ACTIVITY. YOU DON'T BUY THE ART IN THE COLLECTION AND THEN
> OWN IT. THE COLLECTION OWNS A LITTLE
> BIT MORE OF YOU EACH TIME YOU ADD TO IT."
>
> —JOSHUA BAER

Ideas for starting collections come from just about anywhere. We begin by acquiring a single item because it delights us. I bought an old catcher's mask at a show once, and then I began to notice others. They evoked memories of playing baseball as a kid, all the good times playing catch with Dad. I began to enjoy the act of seeking out good examples, and I started to gather them up. The quality of my catcher's masks and the pride I take in them today are functions of my emotional connection to what I collected.

At other times we come across a gathering of items, variations on a theme, like a group of soda pop bottles. We are reminded of summer days long ago, and we are charmed. A collection is started because we have been shown how to make a common object resonate in multiple. Some of the most interesting ideas begin this way, with the most common elements: sports ticket stubs, matchbook covers, bottle caps, refrigerator magnets.

If you enjoy the investment appeal of collecting, I suggest you do two things. First, be attentive to something of unique cultural significance happening right now that could be of value or interest in the future. A good example of this is the growing interest today in rock-art posters from the 1960s. Second, look for collectibles that have nostalgic appeal, but may still be slightly out of fashion. You can use antiques shows as a gauge to confirm your instinct for things that are undervalued—they'll be plentiful and still not too expensive. Themes and personal interests provide the best sources for ideas. Take your favorite room in the house and collect something that can be displayed there. Build a collection around different examples of a handcrafted form, like burlwood bowls or corkscrews. If you love a shade of the color blue, then build a collection around everything you can find in the same color. Shapes and forms repeated in series are marvelous to study. In the end, be open to the world around you, and the ideas will flow. Collecting will become a part of you and your home.

Still Lifes

**"I WANT TO REACH THAT STATE OF
CONDENSATION OF SENSATIONS WHICH
CONSTITUTES A PICTURE."**

—HENRI MATISSE

The practice of visual display in a store like Zona reveals the art in making a still life, which is a composed vignette comprising visually pleasing objects, textural materials, and decorative elements. When we create a still life in our homes, we are deliberate about object placement in the hope that we can visually achieve a whole that is more resonant than its individual parts. Still life compositions are one of the most enjoyable ways to decorate the home and provide ample opportunity to cultivate the eye.

Selecting a good stage is the first step: the mantle above the fireplace, a console table in a hallway or near an entryway, windowsills with a backdrop of natural light, a series of shelves in the living room or library, a vanity table in the bathroom, an open shelf in a kitchen cupboard, a vintage peg rack located at the bottom of the stairs. These spots are examples of locations in which to practice creative still life compositions.

Next, identify the main object, the one that will establish a focal point. Build around it with accent objects of contrasting scale and texture. In one example, you might focus on a large wooden bowl filled with a visual potpourri of textural elements you gathered outdoors. Center the bowl on a table. Step back, take a look, and create symmetry with objects of similar size on each side. A pair of tall candleholders will provide anchoring. Place a small but favorite book on one side. On the other side, place a recently framed photo from a seasonal outing.

Still life compositions can also be fun to do with groupings of decorative elements placed in a series. For example, take five glass cylinders of the same shape and form. Fill them all to the exact same height with an assortment of nuts, seeds, pods, or spices. Line them up in order on a shelf in your living room or kitchen. The repetition of form will highlight the individual element. You can make still lifes like this out of any sort of object you have in multiple: a collection of small clay pots, a series of large pine cones, a grouping of vintage glass bottles. Use a still life series as a fun way to create a centerpiece with flowers or natural materials, instead of employing one single mass in the middle of a table. When paraded in a loose line down the table, those vintage bottles, each bearing a single cornflower or rose, will have visual impact equal to that of a huge bouquet.

USE PEG RACKS AND HOOKS IN ACTIVE ENTRYWAYS TO DISPLAY OFTEN-USED CLOTHING ARTICLES, HATS, AND JEWELRY.
NOTICE HOW THE SIGN HELPS CREATE A THEATRICAL CONTEXT.

THE DRESSED SET

"The dressed set" is a theatrical reference that implies that a stage is totally composed and in waiting, ready to receive the players and the play. We know at Zona that to activate a home we have to prepare it with ceremony and then play within it. When you are decorating a space, whether rearranging the overall placement of furniture or simply hanging holiday adornments, remember that your home is your stage.

AN UNUSUAL PANTRY STORAGE CUPBOARD CREATES A DRAMATIC CENTER POINT IN THIS
ELEGANT COUNTRY DINING AREA.

This element of theater in your space is the key to maintaining formality and objectiveness as you go about the work of making a home radiate character and comfort.

We've created a sort of drill to refer to as you go through the steps of decorating and activating your space. As we explore different room settings you'll see that the equation of variables changes based on the particular functions of the space, but we ask the same questions of ourselves each time, in each room, to achieve the greatest measure of harmony and comfort.

STRATEGIZE THE SPACE

When preparing for any decorating project, make a list of the strategic demands on your space, determine architectural parameters, and try to generate practical solutions—all before you start laying in atmosphere and furnishings. This process will save you a lot of time in trial and error. The information you gather here, about the orientation and role of each room as it relates to the flow of the whole space, will represent the one set of constants you can refer to as you change around the internal composition of your rooms.

SENSUALIZE THE SPACE

Once you have a cursory map of your space laid out, it's time to fill your rooms with sensory elements. Take care to note that while every sense should be invoked in your home, certain spaces will elevate a particular sensory experience above all others. Encourage this when it adds focus

to a room and discourage it when it becomes distracting. Try making a checklist for the senses and apply it to each room, to make sure you have represented each sense sufficiently and woven the separate elements together to create a cohesive atmosphere.

SUPPLY THE SPACE

Material possessions provide the majority of a home's personality. These are the elements least constrained by the rules of space because, major pieces of furniture notwithstanding, they can be moved around at will and serve many rooms equally well. Take care to put your belongings in the context of supply and demand, and work to eliminate or store what you are not currently attached to. Classify your possessions in terms of how you mean to represent them in your home: Is an object a commodity, an essential, an heirloom, or some combination thereof? Do items belong to thematic collections or are they available for still life composition? Pay special attention to those pieces, large and small, that are sacred and need to be displayed with reverence. Make sure you distribute narrative personal items evenly throughout your home.

You are dressing the set of your home completely when you cultivate these three systems in constant and comfortable unison. Home is a place of dynamics that thrives on perpetual and dedicated change, so embrace decorating as a series of experiments, and don't hold on to any set of results too fiercely, successful or failed though they may be. There will always be another chance to build up the shape of a room, and there will always be another chance to tear it down.

Energy Centers

Rooms are energy centers in your home. They hold the echo of all the activities performed within them, and are charged by the histories of the objects that populate them. In our stores we dress raw open space to resemble different functional rooms, and we succeed not because we have all the right parameters in place, but rather because we know how to tell the story of a room. We achieve this through an informed balance of functionally and aesthetically essential furnishings. In a Zona home you will see a dialogue between the rustic and the elegant, the luxurious and the bare, the playful and the serious, the conventional and the unexpected. Since there are actually few rooms in a home that continue to deserve the boundaries of their traditional names, acknowledging this healthy friction—juxtaposing identity and mutability— is what the work of decorating today is all about.

THE KITCHEN

Entering a kitchen is akin to entering the nerve center of most homes. Take a moment to become attuned to the technical sophistication of a kitchen first: The quality of the appliances will tell you a lot about how the space will be used. Pay special attention to countertops and pantries and peripheral shelves because these are the primary spaces dedicated to thematic and decorative elements. Investigate the possibilities for seating, within the space or in close proximity. Evaluate the lighting and color of the kitchen; look for warmth and light-heartedness as in no other room. A kitchen should not be a heavy space, even if it is outfitted for serious cooking. Kitchens are routinely active places, and they should be made to celebrate all that commotion, not hide it.

When looking to improve on your own kitchen, think first about color. We often like to bring bold, saturated color into the kitchen—brightly painted walls, colorful tile accents, dishes and cookware, framed art, and even specialty appliances. Pick a color theme for your kitchen that will allow for some harmonious color mixing. For instance, if you have a prized set of beautifully enameled blue pots and pans that you want to display, select a wall color that will complement them.

If your kitchen can accommodate it, always include a table and comfortable seating within the space. We are particularly fond of odd-sized wooden farm tables with mismatched chairs. Furnishings like these add rustic charm and texture to a room typically filled with smooth, clean lines and surfaces. A table and chairs will encourage informal and intimate dining and make for enjoyable visit-

ing when meals are being prepared. Even in the smallest kitchen, a pair of weathered stools set under a utility counter can provide a sense of welcome and comfort.

Play around in your own kitchen area with furnishings that create a bridge between cooking space and gathering space. Layering personal possessions into an area like this

is an important way to establish that bridge. Think about items like bowls and pitchers, or collections of interesting textiles, that can serve as both presentation pieces in a meal setting and display props for other types of still life: Books—cooking and otherwise—also help personalize this space and create an alternative spot for reading.

Natural elements find a meaningful home in the kitchen, and especially the pantry. Display a box filled with dried herb bundles next to a series of glass jars filled with loose teas. Make a wreath of chili peppers and hang it above the pantry door. Elements like these will have the added benefit of producing a recognizable and comforting aroma in your kitchen.

THE BATH

The bath is a shrine to fragrance and cleanliness. When evaluating a bathroom, always look for elements that make it feel luxurious: beautiful towels, textured floor mats and shower enclosures, sparkling fixtures, inviting scent. Anticipate pale, cool background colors to make the space feel clean. The interesting shapes of specialty or vintage tubs and sinks anchor the space.

Pay close attention to fixtures. If you happen to have a vintage tub or sink, make it the visual centerpiece of the room. You can do this by painting your walls a backdrop color slightly darker than the fixture, or, with an old footed tub, you can paint it the accent color. Tune in also to the functional beauty of tile. This is our favorite construction material for the bathroom because of its durability and relative water resistance. Tile is a great medium for color, and the grid pattern inherent in its installation gives your walls added dynamics.

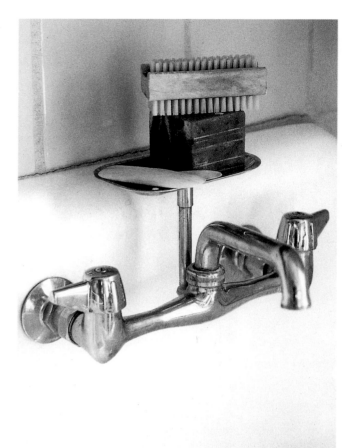

Shelving and storage for extra towels or aromatics give a bathroom texture and character—we like to use clear, clean materials like glass and metal for shelving systems here. Towel racks should be plentiful; we prefer metal. Elevating the quality of secondary fixtures like these will contribute to the visual cohesion of the space.

Whether you're decorating a powder room or a family bath, the mirror is the most important furnishing. You can be thematic and bring in a mirror that is all clean lines and beveled edges, or you can choose a mirror in an opulently decorative frame for contrast. A highly carved gilt or oversized wooden frame will heighten the importance of the mirror within and expand the sense of scale in this often small space.

Your bathroom will hold tiers of scent: soaps, shampoos, lotions, and a fragrant mister. Aromatic candles, bath oils, colognes, powders, potpourri, and scented rosebuds or eucalyptus leaves create a complex recipe for fragrance. Fresh flowers, aromatic or not, will visually anchor the scent of the space.

For adults, bedrooms become havens of quiet and sanctuary; for teenagers and children, bedrooms are exercises in personal expression and places to learn about privacy. When looking at bedrooms, evaluate two factors above all others: the acoustics of the room and the bed itself. These two elements relate most intimately to the rejuvenative success of the space. Decorative and leisurely elements aside, the bedroom has a spartan

the overall style of the room. If you live in a more natural, secluded environment, it is indeed a wonderful option to have no window shades at all, to allow yourself to awaken with the natural rising of sun and sound outside.

Think about the orientation of your bed in the room: Do you need sunlight to wake you up or are you more comfortably awakened in morning shadow? In a nod to feng shui, experiment with the axis on which you sleep. Try setting up

sense of practicality to it. Honor this necessary asylum for sleep by veiling it in luxuries like fine linens and blankets, a private sound system for bedtime music, comfortable seating, and attentive treatments for the light in the space.

In your bedroom, always start with the windows. With thoughtful dressing, they will suppress the primary invasions of light and noise from outside. Opaque curtains or louvered blinds are good buffers and will help determine

your bed first on a north-south, then on an east-west, axis. You may find a considerable improvement in the quality of your sleep depending on what direction you sleep in.

Dress your bed seasonally, so that it remains in tune with the weather and light outside. You can extend the character of your bedroom from the windows and the bed itself by including other fabric elements like decorative pillows, lap blankets, and hanging textiles for the walls.

The bedroom is a haven for fabric. We spend more time lying down, and are in touch with more surfaces, in the bedroom than in any other room. Textiles are also excellent buffers of sound. A bed filled with quilts and pillows will provide you with a quieter sleeping experience than a bed made up less generously.

After your bed is arranged, you should make room for a bedside table. Whether it's a small stool to reach down to,

good to change this pile around frequently, especially as new authors or topics pique your interest. Since lighting for reading is important, you must include a source of it here. Use a lamp with an ambient shade, so the light isn't too sharp, or, better yet, keep a candlestick next to the bed and read at night by candlelight. There's no light more soothing or evocative.

Moving around the rest of your room, take care to bal-

a tall narrow stack of crates holding books, or a finely crafted piece of furniture, the bedside table is best defined by the personal possessions that find their way here: jewelry, alarm clock, photographs, books. We always recommend starting out a bedside with books—not just the one you're currently reading, but a collection of titles that hold wisdom and stories that are dear to you. It's

ance the required systems of storage—case goods, wardrobes, closets—with beautiful accent elements. Drape a beautiful piece of lace or silk over the top of a chest of drawers, and use the space to display a special collection of objects or a jewelry box. Bring scent into the bedroom by displaying your various cologne and perfume bottles on a spare shelf, and use the space as a secondary vanity.

Kids' Rooms

Kids love toys. If you have children, it often seems as if your whole house is overrun with their playthings. In overwhelming moments it's important to remember that even though Barney and Barbie have come to live with you, they need not diminish your home's search for balance. They just need to be put into context. Since it's impossible to hide all the toys away—this stuffed animal or that game will doubtless get pulled out within minutes of its being put on a shelf—you can work at putting storage on visual display. The benefits are twofold for your kids: They enjoy seeing their belongings, and it's easier for them to learn "put it away" habits if they perceive that their things are treated as special.

Children's rooms require plenty of storage, with easy stowaway capacity and quick access. We can achieve this with large decorative, sturdy trunks, with tops that are not too heavy. Long planks of shelving set fairly high around the perimeter of a room provide extra storage and display outgrown but beloved teddys, games, and books. Simple shelving units can be reserved for books, cassettes, and favorite toys of the moment. Small metal athletic lockers work well for sports gear. Closets should be organized and scaled from a kid's point of view. Use plenty of colorful hooks hung on a wall at a height that the child can reach. Coats, hats, outdoor and indoor clothing articles find their home here.

Refrain from cartoonish color schemes around the room: Your children will quickly outgrow whatever motifs you put before them. Flexibility in room aesthetics is essential. Maintain the "green" theme in your child's room as much as in any other part of the home. Give kids an immediate introduction to the world of plants and nature. Find ways to bring natural materials into their rooms wherever possible. Help them grow their own pot of bulbs or catalog a bunch of different minerals or keep a fish in a pretty bowl. Keep interesting books about the earth, the stars, and the animal kingdom intermingled with their favorite stories. There are many natural science books being written for children, and they are often wonderfully illustrated.

Just a small tasting of old things placed in a child's room elevates the aesthetic of the whole environment. You can decorate the space with vintage toys and antique children's books, which provide a textural counterbalance to the many contemporary toys and dolls made out of colder materials. Precious dolls and books from older children's younger days should have their spot as well: These become heirlooms to hold on to as they grow up. Finally, assign a wall or panel where young children can hang their own drawings, for this encourages them to think about themselves and their space artistically.

OPPOSITE: KIDS LOVE TO MAKE CHAOS OUT OF ORDER. OUR CHILDREN LEARN THIS WAY. MAKE THE HOME A SETTING WHERE, OUT OF THE CHAOS, ORDER IS RESTORED AND A SENSE OF HUMOR CAN BE MAINTAINED.

The Dining Room

At Zona, the dining room is a flexible space. The act of eating together defines any space holding the appointed table as a dining room. This means that the architecture of a dining room is much less important than the material aspects of the space. Look for beautiful, heirloom furniture in this room—a table and chairs, of course; a sideboard; a step-back cupboard to display your fine dishes, silver, and glassware. A real dining room may not be the only place you eat in at home, so try to raise the standard of this space to accommodate a more formal and festive kind of meal. Treat the dining room table as the hub of celebration in a home, whether or not there are any guests.

To assess dining room space in your home, first decide if the room in which you will place your big furniture will be performing other roles as well. For instance, we've seen many people set up one end of a large dining room table as a provisional office, with room made in a sideboard or cupboard for storage of mail and other supplies. The family table is also a good place for the kids to do their homework. A pair of closely huddled chairs at one end, sporting decorative pillows or a draped shawl, results in an unexpected spot for intimate conversation. Since you always want to grow into this type of room in terms of entertaining and family, it is wise to buy furniture larger than what you may need at present.

Atmosphere rates in importance second only to the quality of your furniture in a dining room. Candlelight and chandelier light are special here. Thematic music helps raise the mood of the room. Favorite pieces of art—especially paintings—should be hung on the wall, to set a standard of sophistication. Space for display of food and flowers should not be restricted to the table. We love the tradition of the sideboard, or buffet, as an additional presentation spot in this room. You can install a thick shelf of glass or stone with wrought-iron sconces here, use a long console table, or invest in a classical sideboard with built-in cabinetry. If you live in a home with an open plan, a long, low piece of furniture like this divides space nicely, and suggests a boundary between the activities occurring on either side. For visual weight complementary to a big table, we are fond of sideboards made of wood. Antique painted versions, like hunter's tables and dry buffets, are often our favorite vintage buys.

Setting a dining room table is almost a ritual of home for Zona. We recommend instituting it as a tradition even when you are not entertaining, because it invests the daily ritual of family dining with new importance. A well-designed table should be a symphony of contrasting shapes, colors, and textures. The individual elements do not need to be your finest; in fact, setting a table with your daily dishes makes the typical a lot more special. Always include an organic component, like bowls of visual potpourri parading down the middle of the table or an informal pitcher of flowers or a vintage apple-picking basket filled with seasonal vegetables. Placemats of jute or denim or bundled twigs add character and help anchor all the pieceware on top of them. Be adventurous in your mix of materials: A tabletop can absorb glass, ceramic, metal, wood, and fiber all at once.

THE GUEST BEDROOM

When you can afford to dedicate a private room to houseguests, take care that you provide all the same amenities for them that you would for yourself. Clear out any personal clutter and keep the space understated. Make sure you furnish your guests with high quality bedding: a good mattress, fresh pillows, clean and comfortable sheets, and extra blankets. Encourage them to truly unpack and inhabit the room by including scented sachets in a chest of drawers or filling the closet with fine cedar hangers. Leave them their own set of towels at the foot of the bed. On their first night in your home present guests with a bouquet of flowers or a small potted plant they can take away with them. Sensitive and gracious hospitality like this creates good will in your home and deepens its sense of welcome and comfort.

The Home Office

It's a fact of modern life that work gets done at home. More and more it seems, we need to dedicate a room to all our computer equipment, our files, papers, and correspondence. This room is our home office, and clutter is at its greatest here. A home office does not need to be a large room; it just needs to have lots of shelves and drawers and cabinet space. Built-ins are great, while

is a room, like the kitchen, where you can explore wall color and move away from neutral tones. Always provide additional lamp light for a work space; overhead lighting is usually too diffused. You may want to set up two different areas with separate sorts of lighting—one for writing, at a desk, and one for reading, chair-side.

The desk is an essential piece of furniture in your home.

bookcases and tall, standing cabinets are almost always helpful additions.

Whether or not you work out of your home, it is important to make a special space for the intellectual life of your family. Because of the coldness of electronic equipment, try to furnish this space as warmly as poosible.

After assessing your storage situation in a home office, move immediately to a manipulation of color and light. Place your desk underneath or near a window, so you have a natural frame of reference to counterbalance the static shapes of books and blotters or the stark screen of your computer. Make sure you have plants and flowers in this space to bring the palette of nature inside. In addition, this

You can easily make your own desk out of functional components like filing cabinets and butcher block, or you can look for an old-fashioned desk with lots of drawers. The Zona alternative is to use a medium-sized table as a desk and build storage above it. This choice affords you a much higher level of aesthetics in your office and gives you far more leg space for comfortable seating. A table also provides the opportunity to establish more than one work station, so you can turn away from one sort of task and approach another from a fresh perspective. Our favorite desks are heavy, sturdy pieces, usually made out of wood (ponderosa pine or mesquite) or a combination of stone and wood.

The office is one place in a home where you should really

depend on bookshelves filled with books. In this age of technology, books are a grounding influence and give an office needed sensuality.

Amenable seating in a home office is often an afterthought. To remedy this situation, start out with chairs from other rooms that are tried and true. As with your desk, choose chairs for both looks and comfort. Keep more than one chair in the space, to encourage the invited con-

When you hang these items, always measure up from the top of your desk instead of centering them on the wall. Drop everything down a little lower than you normally would to compensate for the fact that much of your viewing will be done from a sitting position rather than standing.

The tabletop and shelving surfaces of your office will no doubt hold an odd mixture of junk, utensils of the trade (pens, pencils, paperclips), and still life objects. Everyone

versation or impromptu meeting. The chairs needn't match each other, or the table, as long as they're made out of complementary materials. Two of our favorites are vintage chrome chairs with recovered seats and rustic farm chairs painted bright colors. To maintain independent space around your reading area, make surprising furniture choices. Bring in a comfortable rocker or an overstuffed loveseat with lots of pillows.

Pay close attention to the floors and walls of your office. Lay down a special rug, both as a soundproofing agent and a textural anchor. Take care to hang photographs and collections around the walls of your office. These elements will keep the office integrated into the home life of your space.

needs a space for junk: Somehow we find it helps us remain more organized everywhere else if we have at least one place to throw scraps of things we're not quite ready to dispose of. Keep one drawer in your filing cabinets or use a handsomely crafted box that will not betray its contents atop your desk. This type of box also serves to vary the dynamic of your table surface, since you can pedestal things on top of it. Indeed, two junk boxes make very good bookends for small volumes like atlases and diaries that you may want to keep out for easy access. The work surfaces of your office should in this way resemble a well-thumbed-through book: pages folded down, turns of phrase underlined and highlighted for inspiration, gracefully used and delightful in mess.

PHILCO
1238

King of all two-door refrigerators,

the luxurious 12 cubic foot Philco "Automatic"

with 2½ cubic foot built-in Master Freezer.

$199.95

At Home with Technology

"WE DON'T HAVE TO HIDE THE TV IN THE ARMOIRE ANYMORE.
MACHINES—COMPUTERS, FAXES, STEREOS—ARE PART OF LIFE.
THEY CAN EXEMPLIFY STUNNING MODERN DESIGN. WE
USE THEM CONSTANTLY, AND IT'S INCONVENIENT, AS WELL AS
POINTLESS, TO PRETEND THEY'RE NOT THERE."

—JAMES MANSOUR

The Industrial Revolution has provided recent generations with the tools to replace a lot of the hard labor of human muscle. The invention and proliferation of machines did the work and provided the fuel for a long period of economic expansion and prosperity. This revolution also helped the growing middle class to think about their homes in terms of efficiency and created a market full of helpful appliances.

I remember quizzing my grandfather once, asking him what he thought was the most important invention of his lifetime. I was sure it would be something essential, like the telephone or the television. He looked at me without pause and said, very matter-of-factly, "The Frigidaire." "Why?" I asked. He responded with a vivid memory: "Lou, before we had an icebox in our home I would have to go downstairs, four flights every day, and meet the local ice man at his ice truck, and I would have to carry that ice back up four flights of stairs before my mom got home from work." The introduction of the refrigerator was certainly a formative influence on the life of my grandfather because of the time and labor it saved him. His personal experience underlines how amenities we take for granted today were in his time major events in the development of the home. I learned right there that as technology intercedes in the routines of the household, for better or for worse, it's important to take note of what's being replaced. The waves of machinery that were introduced to save time certainly did so, but they also began erasing a lot of the human touch in our homes.

The information revolution is now doing to the mind what the Industrial Revolution did to the muscle. As computer technologies come home, making the chores of work ever easier, the knowledge base of traditional home-making is being lost under the weight of disinterest and distraction. We tune into our computers, and tune out the rest of our space. Today, with electronics and the multimedia disciplines gaining irrefutable footholds in our homes, I try to pay close attention to those activities I've given up and, whether I liked performing them or not, revive them every once in a while to remember how far we've come in such a short time.

A good way to manage technology in the home is to make sure that for every gadget or appliance you've got, you also keep around something close to its hand-run counterpart. In your home office, keep some beautiful pencils and a thick ream of paper by your computer or typewriter and write a few lines down by hand each time you use the machine. You can start a journal of your musings and doodles. Or hand-write a letter to a friend instead of sending e-mail. Simple revertings like these to the old-fashioned way of doing very elemental tasks helps keep the home in balance. They encourage a dialogue between the old and new that will help us be better friends to both.

FOR MANY, THIS PHILCO 1238 REFRIGERATOR WAS THE MAJOR TECHNOLOGICAL INVENTION OF ITS TIME.

The Family Room

Make sure there is a space in your home for family. It's important to offset the casually communal routines of your home's nuclear population from both the more public spaces in which you entertain and the more private spaces to which you retreat. The family room is a soft room, with very comfortable furniture and lots of visual souvenirs. The point of reference from which you radiate out should be a fireplace. If you don't have one, think about installing a mantelpiece to create a surrogate hearth space.

In most rooms we advise the sketching of the space in broad strokes, but in the family room it's best to jump right in with your precious objects and dress the mantelpiece first. This will almost surely determine the orientation of your furniture, so think about what you can hang on the wall above your mantel to focus attention. If you have an interesting structural feature here like exposed brick, play it up as much as possible with dramatic lighting, and keep the presentation of objects sculptural and spare.

Color can move toward vibrancy or neutrality in the family room, depending on how the space interacts with the rooms surrounding it. Family area is often distributed into part of a larger living room, for example, or can open onto a kitchen. Make color selections for the walls accordingly, before you choose fabrics for the upholstered furniture in the space.

We really like creating seating areas for family space out of a smaller sofa and a larger number of individual chairs. An ensemble of seating pieces encourages people to face each other and interact, and also creates better dynamics of texture and mass. Try anchoring a space with a sofa upholstered in solid fabric, and surround it with both stuffed and framework chairs. Mix materials, mix solids and patterns. Earth-toned leather, linen, canvas, and chenille are all great upholstery options for this type of space. Stay away from very formal fabrics: If you want texture. look for a solid cotton damask where the pattern is in the weave. Make sure you have lots of pillows and lap blankets, and store them in decorative baskets on either side of the sofa.

The compass of a family room always spins around a low, central gathering table. This table is the site of informal meals, intimate conversations, and many beautiful books and objects. At Zona, we always illuminate this table by candlelight. Try using a collection of five or six candlesticks scattered about the table, or find a few larger ones that are pedestaled above the surface of the table on stands.

Create visual storage in this area by selecting a table with a bottom shelf, and by artfully placing stools and chests around the periphery of the arrangement. Our best gathering tables are made of wood, both rustic and painted, or of glass and stone on iron bases. A wonderful way to customize this type of table is to have a box form built with a recessed surface, covered by a piece of glass. You can fill the gap with river rocks, dried flowers, pine cones, beach glass, or a single beautiful piece of embroidered cloth, to create an illusion of texture right under your fingertips. This system is flexible, so try changing the elements inside every few months to reflect the season.

The wide collection of equipment that makes up a home's media and entertainment systems is often housed in the family room. The ability to conceal that equipment when it's not being used is an important tool in retaining the human balance of this room. Built-in cabinetry and portable entertainment centers are appealing ways of hiding or at least consolidating all these electronics; retrofitting a vintage armoire is another way to keep the fixtures of the room in harmony with your other furnishings. As important as the media have become, and as much as we draw pleasure from big screens and great speakers in our homes, it is helpful to not centralize this room on the apparatus. We extinguish a degree of human interaction when we can all enter a room and become more engaged by the television than by one another. We further help balance out the recreational landscape of the family room by keeping many hands-on board and parlor games there, including dominoes and cards. Remembering the spirit of the hearth will keep us true to the real source of comfort in that space—the kinship of family.

FURNITURE DESIGNER-BUILDERS, ANTHONY HAGEN AND MARK LEVINE OF LONG ISLAND, ACHIEVED A HANDSOME SOLUTION TO THE CYBER STORAGE CHALLENGE. THE CABINET IS FUNCTIONAL AND COMPLEMENTS THE EXISTING SURROUNDINGS THROUGH THE USE OF MAHOGANY AND BIRCHWOOD PANELING.

The Living Room

The living room, where you entertain, is the most theatrical space in your home, so look here for a heightened sense of drama in the presentation of your furnishings. Everything has a proper place in the living room; it is very nearly gallery-like in that the space should be subordinate to the objects you want to show in it. The way to evaluate this room is to see whether the items on display, including furniture, have been given a rich context to live in.

A Zona living room is simply a place to show off one's most precious possessions. The beautifully contoured sofa, the collection of Indian baskets, the antique carpet, the cultivated orchid—all cohere because of the singular eye that picked them. Accordingly, you don't need to arrange this more formal room along set period or ethnic lines unless you want to. Let the room be eclectic if the things you love are eclectic.

We tend to design living rooms with a high contrast of dark and light tones. For example, if your furnishings are heavy and colorful, then the setting should be substantially neutral and pale. If you have collected pieces of furniture and art in subtle, earth-inspired tones, then you can play around with a more dramatic background of richly treated windows and a darkly patterned rug or floor. Overhead lighting is truly critical in this room, as you will surely want to spotlight different items around the space. Scent should be consistent and distinctive. Try

creating a special mister or potpourri blend for this room.

The furniture in this space can be a little more elegant than in other rooms of your home and a little more sparse. We like the space to suggest a bit of emptiness, to make room for the additional elements of hospitality you will bring in when you entertain: extra flowers and candles, trays of food and toasting glasses; more resonant music; more people. When the space is empty it should be comfortable enough to invite intimacy; when full, it should be elastic enough to take on the particular mood of the moment.

Your living room should have an inspired mix of personal collectibles and artistic heirlooms. In this way the composition of the interior space is not far from that of the family room: It is in fact a common occurrence in today's homes that one room serves both purposes. When this is the case, try to merge the aesthetic concern of displaying objects with plenty of space around them, with the informal, more integrated approach to family space. Make sure that there is plenty of flexible seating, strong imagery on the walls, warm, layered floor treatments, and inviting passages into other rooms. In this way the living room is a threshold of sorts: It's where we enter and exit the act of entertaining, but it does not harbor the entire experience. The whole of our home's interior does that job for us, when each room is well set up to greet and receive its visitors.

Frames of Reference

THEMES

One of the principles of Zona home design is to organize interior styling around themes. Themes are a flexible frame of reference. Often they provide a general context that you can enter into and identify. For example, one of the overriding themes in our stores is the idea of "international country." The material objects that fit into this framework are always changing. Sometimes our space feels very festively Mexican; other times we bring in major populations of objects from Bali and India. The tone and timbre of the space is altered, but the feeling of cohesive style remains the same.

Start a home workbook for theme inspirations. Always write down your ideas, and do not edit them. Select rooms in your home and think of themes that might influence their design. For instance, in a child's room, you might illustrate a fairy tale, or the idea of the circus. For a bedroom, you might focus on a historical theme. Themes based on color or places you have visited are often highly inspirational. The theme of time, the theme of space, and the theme of light are conceptual favorites with great interpretive potential.

SENSORY ENVIRONMENTS

You can refer to some other constants within your home to serve as a sort of permanent thematic framework. Elemental or cultural environments can strike especially deep chords in our aesthetic sensibility and serve to honor places we've traveled to that have influenced us. There are many environments that possess characteristic palettes, evoke distinctive soundscapes, and in general stimulate our senses in a very specific way. Try thinking about your home as a tribute to the aesthetics of an environment like the seaside, the mountainside, the desert, or even a particular city.

For example, if you love the beach, maintain a painted palette of neutrals with great blue accents, and pay much attention to the creation of warm, illuminating light. Bring natural materials into your home that transport you back to the seaside: piles of sand and shells for visual potpourri; a sculptural piece of driftwood in still life with some natural sponges and aromatics in your bath; breezy layers of fabric instead of single weighty coverings. Mix outdoor, wicker, and bamboo furnishings in with your more traditional furniture, and install ceiling fans for evocative atmosphere and favorable air circulation. When you begin to create a picture of any environmental interior, refer back to your home checklist and mission statement, and use other influences and goals you've gathered there to help you implement your theme.

SEASONS

The seasons are more of a constant than anything else in the home and can be celebrated thematically. The best way to do this is not to try to re-create a season within your home, but to make decorative changes in tune with external light and color every few months. This practice will help keep your space active without letting it succumb to overly traditional interpretations of the seasons and the holidays that accompany them. If you live in a warm weather climate with no major season changes, this sort of framework can especially help you enliven your space.

The first thing to do to change over your home with the season is to replace all natural elements, including the types of fresh flowers you display. Pay more attention to color than traditional form: For example, if you want a rich red element to symbolize cold weather, make a wreath of chilies or dried red rose heads. You can also head over to your local farmer's market and make a collection of all sorts of herbs and seasonal produce with which to decorate. Invent a new mixture of room fragrances that includes your favorite warm or cool scents. Change textiles around to produce new color themes, and do the same with candles. When you raise up the seasons in your home, you are helping your space maintain balance and forcing out stale sensory experiences. This theme works well as an underpinning for other frames of reference and should be reinterpreted every time an old season rolls around again.

Holidays

uilding-block themes like natural environments and seasons feed directly into Zona's conception of holiday. Holidays are the formal embodiment of a celebration we want our homes to hold every day. The gathering of family and friends is explicit in the remembrance of important religious milestones, historical events, and tributes to special personal days. We believe the same sense of celebration is diffused into every informal visit and each shared meal. Holiday is our most gracious theme for the home.

At Zona, the calendar holidays are moments to dress ourselves up, revisit traditions, and seek a fresh perspective on decoration and style. The spring holiday season begins in April and reaches a climax in May with Mother's Day. We express the coming out from the indoors, to fresh air and the first flowers from the garden. It is the seasonal period to feel the earth, the holiday of renewal. The winter holiday season begins in November, just after Halloween. It reaches a milestone with our American Thanksgiving and extends itself

through Christmas and New Year's. It is our time to highlight the presentation of the natural and textural indoors. We decorate with an eye to elegance and grace. This is the season of gifts and expressions of thanks.

Dedicating a stronghold of energy to holiday seasons helps remedy the disposable sensibility of modern life. When we look at the holidays as a period of time, we maintain a deeper investment in our decorative activities and create context for the many social obligations we find ourselves contending with. We enrich our relationship to tradition and home by personalizing the display of holiday spirit.

Children should be encouraged to contribute to holiday decorating with small, attainable assignments. Use the holidays to teach the value of making a home beautiful. When the entire family is involved, the execution of holiday style becomes significantly more imaginative and personal and is an occurrence to be remembered with pride and affection.

OPPOSITE: CANDLES ARE A CONSTANT COMPANION IN THE ZONA HOME. ALTHOUGH IT IS THE GLOW OF THE LIGHT THAT ILLUMINATES OUR ROOMS, IT IS OFTEN THE AURA OF THE LIGHT THAT ELEVATES THE SPIRIT FOR CELEBRATION.

HOW TO | Decorate for the Holidays

HOW TO MAKE A HOLIDAY POMEGRANATE ORNAMENT

This elegant ornament has become a Zona classic. It's natural, festively colored, and easy to make. Use this simple set of guidelines to create this and other ornaments with your own favorite dried materials.

LIST OF MATERIALS

2 dried pomegranates
Gold or silver spray paint
Glue gun
Floral wire
6 preserved ficus leaves
Cinnamon sticks or small pine cones
20-inch length of 1/2-inch-wide gold-wired ribbon

Spray pomegranates lightly with gold or silver paint. Use hot glue to attach floral wire to the top of each pomegranate. Then, with the hot glue, attach the leaves and cinnamon sticks or pine cones to the top of the pomegranate pair. Let the piece set for about 5 minutes to ensure a strong bond.

Cut an 8-inch length of the gold ribbon and hot-glue it in a loop to the top of the pomegranates. Take the remaining ribbon and make a bow to place on the front of the two pomegranates. Your ornament is ready for hanging.

Decorating for the winter holidays is a special way of saying thank you to our homes. Indeed, the holidays are about celebrating the joys of home. When we decorate our homes for the holidays, we carry out special activities and add new meaning to some of our normal routines. We lay out and place more candles for evening ambience. We set aside wall or mantel space to receive holiday greetings. We think a little bit more about creating a festive tabletop centerpiece. We find a place to write cards and wrap gifts. We open our homes up to friends and family more than at any other time of year.

Here are some tips for how to decorate your home during the holiday season.

1. SELECT SPECIAL SPOTS FOR DECORATIVE ELEMENTS

Select focal points for the placement of textural and decorative elements. Entryways are important starting points. Fireplace mantels remain wonderful shrines for holiday decorating. Select a series of shelves in the living room and kitchen where holiday still lifes can be created and accented with textural decorations. Centers of tables make excellent visual points of concentration. Windowsills and borders are always fun to spruce up. Every home has its special spots.

2. ESTABLISH YOUR COLORS

At Zona, winter holiday colors are faded gold and aged platinum. We stay away from shiny metallics. Our color strategy for years has been based on precious minerals and metals: emerald, ruby, burgundy, forest green, and shades of white continue to be our favorites.

3. ESTABLISH YOUR THEMES

The holidays are fun when thematic. The Italian countryside with a touch of the Renaissance is a long-time favorite. Old Mexico accented with cathedral candles from Spanish monasteries is another. Staying natural and being environmentally friendly during the holidays is a theme we revisit every season. Holiday traditions from cultures other than our own can be festive and add universality to our own decorating. For example, every year I visit the narrow streets of Chinatown to find little novelties for one of my favorite themes, the color of Christmas red. Traditional Chinese have no particular interest in Christmas, but they love the color red. I look for flannels, tin boxes, cookies, and small dolls, and bring these elements into the company of more traditional ornaments.

4. HONOR A HOLIDAY FAIRY TALE

Whether we have children or not. the winter holidays are about great stories. Celebrate a different one each year. *The Secret of the Gnomes*, *The Velveteen Rabbit*, *The Little Prince*, and *Pinocchio* are just a few of our favorites.

5. LIGHTING

Holiday lighting is the most significant design element to create a festive mood and atmosphere. Special elements and more dramatic home lighting must be brought together. Small strings of white lights harbor the spirit of celebration as they trim windows, weave through garlands and wreaths, and are placed around a few other strategic spots in the home like a showpiece mirror or a mantel. Long-burning tall cathedral candles in white and honey are wonderful for central placement on a console or coffee table. Burn them each evening when you arrive home. Place small scented votive candles in your bathroom and by each bed.

6. ORNAMENTS

Holiday ornaments have largely outgrown the single purpose of hanging on trees. The design and making of ornaments at home can inspire a wide variety of placements and displays. Arrange ornaments in bowls on a table, or adorn mantels and moldings. Small homemade ornaments of glass and beads are wonderful dangling along the edge of a living room lamp shade.

7. WREATHS, SWAGS, AND GARLANDS

Textural wreaths, swags, and garlands incorporating dried floral materials signal warmth and welcome in a home. The traditional round wreath made of pine needle leaves (or one made of boxwood. cedar, or bay leaves) is accented with a variety of inviting elements to heighten the style and express the message of welcome and good cheer. At Zona, we accent with ribbon bandings, Australian rose cones, whole chestnuts, miniature dried oranges and woodfruit, and dried flowers, both on the stalk and by the bloom. A host of textural elements can contribute to the recipe or one element can be used alone to extremely elegant effect. We love weaving garlands with strips of old cotton and silk. Store them up and use them in different combinations each holiday.

8. OUR HOLIDAY TOOL CHEST

Colorful assortment of silk, cotton, paper, and organza ribbons

Dried flowers, especially roses, for gift wrapping

Vintage fabrics cut in long strips

Hammer and a wide inventory of picture hooks in different sizes

Glue gun

Framing wire

Push pins and tacks

Natural wrapping materials: papyrus, bark, muslin, canvas, vintage ticking fabric

Bundles of raffia

Sponge and crackle glazing paint

Forged iron hooks

Storage containers or large gift boxes, to preserve holiday decorations

HOW TO MAKE A HOLIDAY WINDOWBOX SHRINE

1. Find an old inexpensive small picture frame (about 2 by 3 inches) at a junk shop or flea market.

2. Spray-paint the frame antique gold or platinum. If you want something more substantial, try real silver or gold leafing.

3. Attach hanging wire or framer's string just below the top of the frame.

4. Tie strings of beads, tarot, and holiday blessing cards from the wire.

5. Hang the frame on a clean wall over a console table.

6. Place three votive candles on a plate nearby for daily lighting.

HOW TO | Make a Spirit Gift

Celebration at holiday time goes hand in hand with a sense of hospitality. Invitations are extended and received between family and friends. A gesture of thanks and appreciation on the part of the guest adds tremendously to the grace of these shared moments. This sort of intimate acknowledgment becomes a wonderful symbol of our relationships and helps to keep the home special as the site of our gatherings. We like to give "spirit gifts" to mark almost any occasion of time shared with friends, and we make special efforts to create them around holidays. These are quiet, small gifts that resonate all the more because of the time and energy spent creating them.

After dinner at a friend's house, take time to compose a letter of thanks instead of just calling the next day. Write your note on beautiful paper and use a calligraphy pen to address the envelope so it looks like something really special. Make the note an acknowledgment of the richness of your friendship.

Make up a traditional bag of cooking herbs from your own garden, or from your local farmer's market, as a hosting gift. Tie a bundle of sprigs together and wrap them in cheesecloth with a few strands of raffia or some pretty ribbon. Attach a dried rose or a few fresh sprigs of herbs to the outside of the package, and you've created a gift as beautiful as it is practical. You can even include a handwritten recipe for one of your favorite dishes using the herbs.

Give someone special a lucky penny you found. Slip it into their hand unexpectedly when you meet for a visit or wrap it in a pretty little Chinese silk pouch stuffed with scented cotton.

Invite yourself to someone else's house to make them dinner. Arrive in the afternoon so that you can visit over a cup of tea while you unpack the groceries and prepare the meal. Make sure you are familiar with your friend's kitchen so that you can bring any missing implements with you. At the end of the meal, after you've done the dishes, leave behind something special, like a beautiful bar of chocolate or the infused vinegar you brought to cook with.

Offer to take a friend's or sibling's child out for a day of holiday adventure, and let the parent have an afternoon of solitude. Organize the event ahead of time so that your day is structured: Go to a museum or to the zoo or for a long walk in the park. Encourage the child to find some simple memento, like a leaf or a feather or a postcard. When you bring it back home, sit down with the child and his or her parents and write the story of your day together. Attach the souvenir to the top of the page to help reinforce a sweet memory of the outing.

Make up small boxes of potpourri as hosting gifts. Save old jewelry boxes and cover them with pretty rice paper. Then fill the boxes with cedar chips and dried flowers and lavender. Or take some nonscented textural item like small pine cones and perfume them with a favorite essential oil. Every time the box is opened, the gesture of friendship in which it was given will reveal itself in fragrance.

To mark a special occasion, give a close friend your copy of a book you especially loved. Write a special inscription memorializing the shared reading experience. Encourage the recipient to pass the book along to someone else when they have finished living with it and reading it.

Take a cutting from your favorite plant and root it for someone. Go to any garden store and find a pretty seed package—preferably for the kind of plant you're giving—and attach some blank paper stock to the back of it. Use this as a card and write down all the care instructions here. Attach this with a bit of raffia to the rim of the pot.

Surprise a friend or family member on their birthday with a bunch of horoscopes cut from various city papers and magazines. Buy a very pretty oversized envelope, slide the horoscopes in, and fill it up with glitter or flower petals, to make a fantastic little token present.

In learning the art of spirit gifts, you are well on your way to creating your own blueprint for a new sort of celebration in the home. Make a celebration every year out of the first snowfall or first rain after a drought. Turn Sunday brunch among friends into a round-robin tradition. Have real birthday parties, replete with cake and candles and decorations, even if you are a grown-up. Activities like these redefine the home both emotionally and philosophically and help us reinvest in the craft with which we all embellish our space and our lives. This is how we pass comfort along from one generation to the next.

In the Element of Fire

Spring

Fire is heat, light, color, and intense power. Fire is also will, a symbol of a life force that seems at once transitory and eternal. The hearth harbors the fire in our homes and invites us into the reflected light of community. It is harnessed to keep us warm, illuminate darkness, cook our food, and convert raw materials into tools for everyday life. It is the most transcendent and yet most practical of elements.

AN INDIAN BEAD MAKER DISPLAYING HIS CRAFT IN A MARKET STALL.

India

India is a country of amazing paradox. Every region of the Indian subcontinent has its own distinct character and craft specialties. There are the masterful textiles and carpets of Kashmir and Pushkar in the north; the gems and blueware ceramics of Jaipur in the northwest; the forged-iron and copper-making workshops outside of Bombay in the southwest; the delightful hand-loomed cotton fabrics of Madras in the south; the incense and sandalwood of Mysore and the delicious spices of New Delhi near the heart of the country. I love the saturated, almost mystically intense color that per-

vades so many of the decorative crafts from this land.

Every visit to India is a pilgrimage, a journey to the roots of ancient tradition and artistry. It is a country whirling in frantic street life, yet seeking peace and stillness at its center. India shows us the colors of fire in its enormous diversity, the energy and heat of flame in its pressing sense of humanity. Here we need not look too far for the artisan, for every person is ignited with an artisan spirit. The craft of hands in meditation or at work is a lasting legacy in this ancient and beautiful land.

4

Hitting the Road

Trade

The assimilation of different styles into a core aesthetic is the traditional result of cultural exchange. Travelers bringing goods back from foreign lands have always greatly influenced the development of their native cultures, in disciplines ranging from art to architecture to fashion to cuisine. I have always seen home in this way, as a native culture, a base camp awaiting the arrival of new information and design intelligence. Tracing the trade routes in the history of your own home—identifying the places you've been or longed to visit that have influenced your sense of style—helps you clarify and enrich your home's mission. In this way, a home is linked as much to the cultural as to the natural. ❡ Over time, travel helps collections get built, heirlooms acquired, and special pieces from disparate origins all look like they fit together: Each item individually serves your interests and your core conception of home. In addition, building a style by finding new ways to highlight exotic materials helps your space recount many layers of history at once. The luxurious stroke of silk in an antique embroidered fragment from Afghanistan; the well-worn scultpure of an African wooden headrest: these traditional objects are transformed by their use—now as a pillow face or a pedestal for a vase of flowers—without diminishing the sense of discovery that brought them into your home. ❡ I believe America is a perfect melting pot for this type of *interior design. It has always embraced and will continue to assimilate the ethnicity of different domestic objects into something new and different. This is why, for example, a vintage Deco armchair from France, all buttery leather and fine patina, looks so well on a rustic carpet from Northern India, or why a classic Shaker farmhouse chair seems so at home in a modern urban interior—the Zona home threads and layers these diverse influences into one seamless presentation. For example, I love an object whose origins are hard to determine—a bowl, perhaps, whose pattern seems to be Southwestern, but whose terra-cotta clay convinces me that it was actually made in Italy. What becomes primary about this piece is the universal resonance of its craft. The evolving style of the Zona home replaces the direct ethnicity of objects with an international transcendence. Add your own distinct family heirlooms and belongings to pieces from other places, and you begin to have an aesthetic for the interior of the home that has its birthright in America but speaks for an international sense of community.*

Routes

The Mission of Travel

At one point or another, we all experience that captivating feeling of being taken over, body, mind, and soul, by a different culture. It is totally invigorating. In my case, I remember my first visit to New Mexico, in 1982. There was something quite extraordinary about the state, and especially the environs around Santa Fe. I wanted to capture the magical quality of the adobe and bring it home to New York. I was ready to throw away all my furnishings at home and replace them with everything Southwestern. I wanted to wear cowboy boots and learn about Native American pottery and weaving. I began to integrate Southwestern materials into my home. The romance was hard to contain: The aesthetic emerged in my color and scent sensibilities as much as it did in the physical objects I brought back with me.

As my travels continued, I learned about other styles and cultures. I began to appreciate the opportunity to complement and fuse the ethnic heritage of one cultural background with that of another. Both Zona and my home became stages for this evolving mosaic, blending the ambience, for example, of the colorful and fresh Tuscan countryside with the dry, earthy, sometimes barren texture of the desert Southwest. The tropical lushness of rich Thai silk fabric was employed to great advantage on a classic English upholstered sofa. Wide Japanese cedar panels were used for flooring. I loved to mix it up.

As my cultural interests evolved, Zona evolved. Framed within a relaxed orientation to the natural, my design aesthetic became a closer representation of how I traveled and how I lived. The mission of travel became for me an exercise in seeing: learning how to document what moved me in a new setting and figuring out how to bring the experience home. Travel gave me the opportunity to collect beauty and inspiration and to weave these elements into my own sensibility. One trip might result in a major piece of furniture, another in little more than a vial of extraordinary scent, or a memory of the ocean's particular shade of blue. All of these documents, major and minor alike, inhabit my home equally.

TRADE ROUTE TOWNS

Towns that I have visited often become symbolic destinations. My favorite towns are the ones that celebrate artisan traditions, value preservation, are beautiful for walking, and kindle my desire to both consume and reflect. Here are my favorites. See if any of them emerge for you as desired travel destinations, and start your own "best-of" list of cities to visit. You can do the same thing with areas of wilderness, too. These frameworks can help motivate you to make a special series of travel albums, or at the very least a cataloguing of slides and photos from the wonderful places you've been.

Florence
Chiang Mai
Jerusalem
Kyoto
Paris
Istanbul
Marrakech
Bali
San Francisco
Hong Kong

When I leave for a buying trip, my bags and my schedule have plenty of space in them. For me, successful traveling means being prepared for serendipity. Wonderful experiences and artifacts are often encountered unexpectedly, so I always allow for the spontaneous side trip or the extra afternoon spent somewhere compelling. I find it wise to gain a rudimentary understanding of a place ahead of time, and then work my way out from center until I'm well immersed in its native rhythms and customs. My perception of the culture I'm visiting is always more penetrating when I move away from an imposed agenda.

I always try to spend part of my first day in a new place with a car and driver. How long I spend getting my bearings in this way is a decision based on time and expense. I like getting started very early in the morning. I enjoy moving around an area quickly at first, making note of spots that I would like to return to and explore: I operate more effectively in unfamiliar surroundings when I have some initial, firsthand orientation and perspective. I ask to see the best shopping streets, the food markets, and places for antiques. I always carry a small pocket notebook to keep tabs on architecture, items, scents, and colors I notice. Sometimes, I have a car or taxi take me to an area I intend to explore and I simply start walking back to where I started. I like to walk in loops and circles. Affording yourself time to meander is a wonderful way to get in synch with a new place, especially cities.

Some of my very favorite experiences in other countries have been predicated on my desire to explore a village known for a particular craft. The best way to get beyond the tourist facade associated with the selling of native crafts is to visit the source of production. I go directly to the village where those lovely baskets are made. I make contact with the artisan whose textiles or ceramics I admire. The trip is always a true a slice of life. If circumstances prohibit me from making personal contact with local artisans, I try to find a dealer who collects directly and who can educate me. I mind my instinct for authenticity and absorb the atmosphere of a place before I begin collecting anything.

Most places have some local specialty or natural feature to recommend them: the wine in Burgundy, the copper pots in Istanbul, the cheese in Parma, the temples in Kyoto, the light at dusk in Jerusalem, the terra-cotta just outside of Florence. I find that every place has the best of something. It may be a taste, a scent, a visual wonder, a haunting sound. It may be a style of craft, a way of painting, or a song to sing. I make it a point to seek that specialness out wherever I go. When I find it, I capture the moment in my travel journal, in photographs, or in collected souvenirs, and bring it home as the prize of my trip.

"MOST PLACES HAVE SOME LOCAL
SPECIALTY OR NATURAL FEATURE TO RECOMMEND
THEM: THE WINE IN BURGUNDY, THE COPPER
POTS IN ISTANBUL, THE CHEESE IN PARMA, THE TEM-
PLES IN KYOTO, THE LIGHT AT DUSK IN
JERUSALEM, THE TERRA-COTTA JUST OUTSIDE
OF FLORENCE. I FIND THAT EVERY PLACE HAS
THE BEST OF SOMETHING."

—LOUIS SAGAR

Seeking the Authentic

Travel is so integrated into the Zona experience of home that we wanted to share with you some of the wisdom we've gained on our own trade routes. Distant travel may not be a possibility for all, but even a day trip to a local antiques market can serve as transport to another world. So much of the joy of home is wrapped up in what we bring back from our travels, near and far, to enrich and beautify the routines of daily life. In travel we are enlightened as we learn how people of different cultures work and live. In travel we are exposed to outdoor landscapes unlike our own. We embrace the disruption of our normal rhythms—we wake up early, eat dinner late at night, walk all day. When we are well prepared, we travel with a relaxed body and a curious mind. We look forward to every part of the journey. It is an opportunity to practice the art of seeing, to find ways of capturing memories, and to bring new artifacts home to share with friends and family.

The Artisan Tradition

THE SPIRIT OF DESIGN

The artisan often acts as a bridge to the understanding of a culture. One of the secrets I have learned from working with artisans is how integrated their work becomes to life itself. The artisan remains the symbol of utility, the maker of the tools for villagers to carry out their daily tasks. The artisan's production is coordinated with the routines of each day, the time of year, and the availability of natural materials. It is this complete integration of craft into the daily life of a community that I have found so inspiring.

I have had the opportunity to travel the world to find wonderful things. It has always been part of my dream to meet remarkable artisans on those voyages and to share their stories. When an example of their work finds a place in our homes, where it can be respected and admired, the artisan's story can unfold and add to our own. Over the years I have visited and worked with countless artisans, small workshops, and production cooperatives. Some tell their stories quite colorfully, while others would prefer to be left alone with their work and their solitude.

I remember some years back, during one of my early trips to New Mexico, when the work of Jim Wagner, a painter in Taos, began appearing in the form of painted furniture. People said that he was a difficult man, hard to get to know, and impossible to do business with. His work was captivating, and I was compelled to track him down. I felt like I was going out to find Jesse James. I think Jim truly appreciated the effort I made to find him. He was full of stories about his previous visits to New York, the big city. Every single piece of furniture made by Wagner in those years sold in an instant. People connected to the spirit of design in the work, even as they embraced its functional use. Jim is an extraordinary and colorful American artisan. If you own one of his pieces, consider it highly collectible.

In the Chiang Mai area of northern Thailand I have spent several long afternoons at the Maya Tongs weaving workshop, where twenty women gather each day to make fine vegetal dyed cotton textiles. It is spellbinding to sit quietly on the floor and listen to the beat of the wooden looms still prevalent in small Thai villages. The rhythmic pulse of the weaving replaces conversation and underlines the soft and silent use of the material they are making. In Italy, I once met up with a young potter in the Umbrian hill town of Todi. Her name was Sylvia. I expressed interest in her lovely style of painting on clay. Within minutes, I was introduced to her mother, also a potter; her sister, who seemed to do a great deal of the cooking; and her grandmother, who lived there too, and would tell stories about the old days. Little children were running around in constant motion. Before I knew it, we were eating. The buoyant gestures of this family were perfectly translated into the ceramics they made.

OPPOSITE: THE CECCARELLI FAMILY SYMBOLIZES THREE GENERATIONS OF ARTISAN TRADITION. SCENES FROM THEIR WORKSHOP CONNECT US TO MAKER AND MATERIAL, BONDING US TO THEIR COLLECTION OF HAND-PAINTED GARDEN TABLES, URNS, AND SCULPTURAL FORMS MADE FROM THE RICH TUSCAN TERRA-COTTA CLAY.

The Endangered Species of Craft

A decorative folk item for the affluent urban dweller is both a useful tool and means of livelihood for the artisan and his family. A good example of this is Zona's classic marble peach. Carlo, an Italian man who has delicately produced marble peaches of extraordinary quality for thirty years, will lament that there is no one to carry on his craft. He sits each day carving and painting his marble collections of fruit. His son has gone to work in the city, and his daughter has no interest in sitting for long days amid the marble dust. When I listen to his story, I want to roll up my sleeves and start carving up the marble myself.

In a little town just outside of Florence, Mario Benci is known as "the master of the clay." His hands have worked the local red terra-cotta clay for forty years. The last time I visited him he told me: "In the old days, there were many small shops along this road, and each one produced terra-cotta. Each shop was known for different forms. During the wine harvest, we would join in the festivities and drink the wine from special flasks made from the earth. Today, we have only a few shops remaining. I myself have no children and no one to carry on my heritage." In my travels I find artisans like these all too often, faced with the dismissal of their livelihoods as old-fashioned, and facing down the

potential extinction of generations-old legacies of craft.

Living in an era when technology is so powerful, we need to maintain balance in our homes by keeping ourselves aware of the feeling of the hand. It's easy to do this when we travel to a foreign place and see the way things are made there. Often, and especially in rural or developing countries, we'll find domestic items made in traditional ways that have extraordinary integrity of material and design. A coconut bowl in Bali, for example, is a useful object because the material is plentiful and easy to manipulate, has excellent water resistant properties, and is beautiful. The artisan tradition teaches us to seek out the best combination of these elements in everything we collect. We preserve an integral way of life, and learn how to better marry beauty and utility in our own, when we give patronage to craft all around the world.

It is our responsibility to make our homes breathe with the spirit of the artisan. When you travel, spend time meeting the artisans of the community. Ask questions, learn about their culture. Demand good design and fine craftsmanship, and you will be shown local products instead of items ready-made for tourists. In the end, you will experience a great deal more of the place you're visiting, and you will have much greater chances of acquiring a meaningful souvenir of your trip.

OPPOSITE: THE RENOWNED ALINARI BROTHERS WERE PHOTOGRAPHERS WHOSE WORK IN THE EARLY 1900S CAPTURED AND PRESERVED THE ABUNDANCE OF ARTISAN WORKSHOPS SO PREVALENT IN THE CULTURE OF ITALIAN LIFE.

Hunting and Gathering

The experience of collecting goods while traveling enriches your memory of a trip and deepens your understanding of a foreign place. I always try to identify a souvenir appropriate to a place I have visited. I never want anything fancy; I always want something memorable. When I arrive at a new destination, I observe what is unique to that place and I also look to see if there are any objects that I might add to a collection I already have at home. For example, I have a friend who loves collecting shot glasses. He acquires one from every hotel he visits. Some have the emblem of the hotel or restaurant, others are shapely and colorful, yet others are basic and spare. This collection is his personal documentation. It now occupies a whole shelf in his study. The shot glasses number over two hundred. When you look at them, they speak with no words. They add warmth and understanding to his home. A simple object, hunted and gathered over years of time.

A lot of the collecting I do for Zona is staged at regional antique fairs. Traveling to a foreign place for me can be as simple as driving out of New York City to visit a local auction house in the Adirondacks—just a few hours away—or hopping on a plane to Texas for a biannual antiques festival in a sleepy Hill Country town called Round Top. Any time I'm collecting "in the field," I consider myself traveling not only to a different place but also to a different time. For a few

DEALERS OFTEN PRESENT THEIR WARES IN DRAWERS AND BOXES. THE HUNTING AND GATHERING BEGINS HERE.

I ENJOY LOOKING FOR GROUPINGS OF COMMON ELEMENTS. THESE GROUPINGS BECOME THE SEEDS FOR FUTURE COLLECTIONS.

hours or days, I get steeped in all manner of things from bygone eras. I find that antiques collecting is one of the most pleasurable ways to identify special pieces for the home. There is always so much to see that little pressure ever exists to find the one "right" thing. I am certain at this point that in the fray, the thing you wish for will always find you.

The last time I visited Round Top, I wanted to foreground some of the key experiences that always make the experience of an antiques buying trip, and that festival in particular, so enjoyable and resonant. Part of it has to do with the location: You couldn't ask for a spot in America more different from New York City. Round Top is located just over an hour outside of Austin, Texas, in a town with one post office, a real town square, a tightly knit community that copes with the crazy influx of visitors twice a year, and miles and miles of rolling landscape filled with wildflowers. There is one road that wanders through town. And surprisingly, there is one world-class café run by a chef and his family who wanted to resettle in their old hometown. The serendipity of a great meal on a warm Texas evening, with real cowboys singing on the porch for those not lucky enough to get a table: This is the quality of the place I've tried to record.

Here is an illustrated version of my journal from that show, with some helpful hints about how to hunt and gather at antiques fairs in general.

The Round Top Antiques Festival

ARRIVAL, TUESDAY EVENING

I am arriving to attend Antiques Week in Round Top, Texas. Dealers from across the country descend upon this small hill country town to participate in a string of shows held in village halls, tent buildings, and along the road in the wide grazing fields. Mildred and Dick Ganchan own the Browning Plantation, an old mansion restored as a bed and breakfast. They have carefully renovated their home over the past ten years as a labor of love, and they welcome me into it in the late hours of the

evening. I've had to fly from New York to Austin, rent a car, and drive down a shady rural route to get here. Round Top is definitely on the road less traveled.

THE FIELD, WEDNESDAY, 6:43 A.M.

The morning light here is amazing. Living in New York, I do not have the chance to see enough sunrises. When I travel in the countryside, I enjoy getting up a little earlier to catch the feeling of the dawn light. There is an early morning palette of colors that always makes an impression on me and allows for an easy connection to nature.

Somehow when I am traveling I find that I am more sensitive to sounds and smells. It is easier for me to be in tune because the environment is fresh to my senses. Over the years, I have found that I can actually concentrate my energy on the particular textural and sense personality of an area I'm visiting. Here in the fields around Round Top, the hill country of Texas is rolling and very open. Home to the blue bonnets in spring and wildflowers throughout the year, I can feel the freshness of the air, and the sense of order in the layout of the land.

A COUNTRY BARN ALONGSIDE THE ROAD, THURSDAY, 8:16 A.M.

I always try to pay attention to how the style of architecture and how well the methods of construction suit a particular environment. Architectural elements, structural details, color and texture, are always worth noting. Keep a small pocket pad and camera handy, and record whatever gives you inspiration and insight. You will be surprised at how much better you recall the whole of a building if you take a little time to document the details

and textures of it. The process will always work its way back into enriching your understanding of a place and will build your confidence in your own development of an interior style. I happen to love barns. They are still-functioning icons of the rural way of life. I always think of them as guest houses for the animals.

THE SETUP, THURSDAY, 9:35 A.M.

I notice all the trucks and vans rolling along the one road into town like a caravan. It seems like every prized possession these folks own is on their trucks. Country

dealers will tell you that the packing and unpacking of their vans requires a system. The hope is that once you unpack at a show, little will be have to be packed up again.

Setup time at shows is a window of opportunity for the dealers to buy from each other. The public is not allowed in at setup. You can hear the chatter of the dealers bragging about this piece or that. Many are already tired from hours of driving and little sleep, but they are energized by the bright sunny day and excited energy from the waiting crowd.

BUD AND KAREN'S APPLE PIE, THURSDAY, 8:30 P.M.

Bud and Karen Royer own the acclaimed Round Top Café. When you taste one of their home-baked pies you become a part of their culture, and you have been welcomed into their kitchen. Here is the real thing. Bud's apple pie and Ronnie Siptak's Texas barbecue are experiences of

authenticity. If you stay curious, open, and imaginative, you can take those experiences home with you.

FRIDAY AFTERNOON, 12:30 P.M.

Walking the rows, lines of them, filled with a wide variety of glassware, ceramics, and items from the attic. Each table depicts the personality of its dealer. In these rows, it is often country women who have carefully gathered each treasure from the homes of friends, and little farm auctions in the countryside. They set their tables with cloths that inspire one to inspect closely the silver and tabletop.

MONDAY MORNING, 8:30 A.M.

The tent is empty, the dealers have packed their vans and trucks, moving on to the next show, returning to their homes. There is a peaceful feeling in the tent. Heirlooms have been acquired, and new friendships have been made.

Preparing the Barbecue

THURSDAY, 11:30 A.M.

Food is the most immediate and direct experience of a people and a place. Every culture has its own "kitchen," a cuisine integral to the rhythm of the culture. I enjoy watching local people prepare local food specialties, especially for large groups of visitors. In small communities, this kind of collective cooking becomes an extension of family. I learn a great deal about the comfort of home by paying attention to the preparation, cooking, and eating of the local foods in cultures around the world.

The Texas barbecue is a ritual of amazing calculation: the making of the fire, the blending of sauces, and the basting of the meat. Ronnie Siptak is a local rancher who always makes himself available to prepare the big barbecue during Antiques Show week. He is a friend of Emma Lee Turney, the woman who started the Round Top Invitational Fair, in a mid-nineteenth-century dance hall, with twenty dealers from the area twenty-eight years ago. Today, Round Top is a gathering of traders and dealers in the hundreds. Emma will tell you that Ronnie Siptak is the only man she would consider to make such an important barbecue. In a sense, Ronnie Siptak is a barbecue artisan, maintaining the tradition, with honor and perfection.

ALBERT KATZ'S BLOOD ORANGE, HONEY AND WALNUT DRESSING

1 tbl. Katz and Company citrus blossom honey
1 tbl. whole seed, grainy mustard
3 tbls. fresh blood orange juice (any orange juice can be substituted)
Finely chopped zest from 1 orange or blood orange
1 tsp. fresh chives, snipped
2 tbls. red wine vinegar
1 tbl. walnut oil
½ cup pure olive oil (not extra virgin), or to taste
Salt and pepper to taste

Place all ingredients, except oils and seasonings, in a bowl and whisk vigorously. Mix walnut oil and olive oil together. Slowly begin to pour the oil mixture into the bowl, gradually adding more oil until an emulsion is formed. Taste for seasoning and adjust accordingly. The dressing should be tart and sweet, and not oily. Add more vinegar to adjust the flavor, if necessary.

Use this flavorful dressing tossed with young spinach leaves, toasted walnuts, blood orange or orange segments, and crumbled goat cheese or maytag blue for a wonderful and seasonal salad. For a richer salad, add cooked, warm pancetta. Enjoy!

Shooting the Breeze

"THERE IS A SPECIAL MOMENT,
WHEN I FIRST SIT DOWN TO TALK TO A TRADER OR
DEALER. IT IS THOSE FIRST FEW WORDS
THAT HELP ESTABLISH A COMMON BOND, A SHARED
INTEREST IN WHAT THEY HAVE TO OFFER,
AND A RESPECT FOR ALL OF LIFE'S EXPERIENCES THAT
HAVE BROUGHT THE TWO OF US TO THIS
POINT OF INTERACTION. A RELATIONSHIP IS FORMED
AND THAT'S THE FUN OF IT."

—LOUIS SAGAR

FRIDAY AFTERNOON, 4:30 P.M.

I have been on the move all day. The buying is best in the morning for the choice pieces, but prices become more negotiable in the afternoon. This is the time of day when I love to sit down and shoot the breeze with a dealer whose eye I like and who might be a resource for me in the future. Harold Raymond is a dealer who finds some of the best wrought iron and garden furniture in the West. He has the best pickers (the people who bring him his stuff), and his prices are always honest. About six miles outside of Round Top, he sets up in a small town campsite. He sits under this big branchy oak tree and hardly gets up out of his rusty old slider chair. If you take the time to sit down with him, you'll be sure to learn a lot, and you'll get a better deal too.

HOW TO | Buy at an Antiques Show

1. DRESS CASUALLY AND IN LAYERS TO ACCOUNT FOR CHANGING WEATHER. If you do any early buying, which often starts at dawn, it will surely be colder in the morning than later in the day. Don't let bad weather prevent you from going to a show; days of rain, cold, and even stifling hot weather are often the days when you'll get the best deals.

2. KEEP A MEDIUM-SIZED KNAPSACK ON YOUR BACK TO STORE ESSENTIALS—water, sunscreen, shed layers of clothing, a notepad, a few pieces of fruit. Discourage any tendency to carry a big bag: It will inevitably get heavy and uncomfortable as it fills up with stuff, and slow you down as you walk the show.

3. ALWAYS WALK A SHOW IN AN ORDERLY FASHION. Keep a crude map of the show layout on hand so that you can mark booth locations where items interested you. Unless you are overcome by love at first sight, take notes and get your bearings over the span of the whole show before you begin doing any serious purchasing. The one exception to this rule is when there is a particular dealer you want to

see. Locate his or her booth on a map of the show, and go visit there first.

4. START YOUR TOUR OF A SHOW FROM THE FAR END OF THE FIELD OR TENT. Most people will enter a fair and start looking immediately down the aisles in close proximity, so there are often many wonderful finds on the peripheries.

5. DIVIDE YOUR FOCUS INTO TWO CATEGORIES: LOOKING FOR THINGS YOU KNOW YOU WANT, AND REMAINING OPEN TO THINGS YOU DIDN'T KNOW YOU WANTED. The best finds at an antiques show are often the most unexpected. If a booth with items not in your usual area of interest draws you in, follow your instinct and take a look around.

6. ALWAYS MAKE INITIAL EYE CONTACT WITH THE SELLER. Initiate a chat about an object you're interested in. If a dealer's eye particularly appeals to you, make an effort to put a grouping together in his or her booth. Multiple purchases—the "package deal"—will often produce a discount overall.

7. MAKE SURE TO EXAMINE ANY PIECE YOU ARE SERIOUSLY

CONSIDERING CAREFULLY BEFORE TALKING TO THE DEALER, to make your own assessment. Learn from the dealer how long he or she has had a piece. Sometimes items that haven't sold quickly enough will go for a better price.

8. **ALWAYS ASK IF YOU MAY TOUCH AN OBJECT.** Feel it; lift it; if it's furniture, take account of the piece's proportions. Sit down at a table; rest for a few moments on a bench or in a chair. Take your time—don't allow yourself to feel rushed into purchasing anything. Keep conversation with the dealer active and positive as you interact with a piece. If you have the time, always sit down to negotiate the price of a piece you're ready to buy.

9. **MOST DEALERS WORK IN TEAMS.** One partner usually is good with logistics and money; the other has the eye. Husband and wife teams normally work that way. The wife has the eye and the husband loads, unloads, and moves the items around. Whatever the circumstance may be, you always want to talk price with the logistics partner. He or she will be less attached to the item and more amenable to making deals.

10. **LEAVE YOURSELF ENOUGH TIME AT THE END OF A MAJOR BUYING SHOW TO CONSOLIDATE AND PACK YOUR MERCHANDISE.** This process will run smoothly and efficiently if you've kept good notes about where you purchased things. It is always money well spent to hire a porter to work with you, especially if you need an outside service to ship your purchases home for you. Locate the show office, and the management there will help you hook up with both porters and shipping agents servicing the show.

11. **DEALERS TEND TO SPECIALIZE.** Their collections will represent a personal point of view and should have a focal area curated with some expertise. Some dealers specialize in a feeling or period: glass from the forties, pottery from certain factories produced in certain years. Others are item and grouping driven. They will show you their collections of tools, dice, children's games, globes, vintage typewriters—you name it. There are some dealers who are collectors themselves and are focused on selling to people who like to collect what they collect. These dealers normally have more knowledge about their field and are often consulted for appraisals and auctions. They appreciate rarity. There are other dealers whom I call "tailgaters." These dealers range from individuals with general interest in an area of decorative antiques to men and women who literally live in their vans, doing upward of forty shows a year, setting up at a new show every week. For example, Bill and Peggy Holstead, who love painted country furniture, are constantly on the road. They buy and sell as they go. I can only get in touch with them by following their schedule of shows. They always have the best stuff, so I make a point of going to the shows where I know they'll be.

Bob Skinner's House

A COLLECTOR'S HOME

It's about 10:30 A.M. and I am about to meet Bob Skinner, a long time collector of carpenter tools, sewing scissors, saws, planes, and tools from the farm. Bob lives with his wife, Liz, in a restored barn on part of an old corn field in the Water Mill area of Long Island. The barn was acquired in upstate New York, before being dismantled and rebuilt virtually by hand on the Skinner property. In Bob's hands, tools are not just simple implements; they are arranged and presented in such a special context that they truly become sculptural folk art treasures. Each of his hammers and scissors has a story. This man's knowledge of his tools makes you feel that he could fix just about anything, and he just might be able to. Bob Skinner collects something he loves and knows about. The comfort of his home resonates with a sense of history and wisdom, preserved in the collections he owns and displays.

Always take the time to get to know dealers you want to work with as friends. A dealer with a high level of expertise in his or her field can help curate a collection that is top quality, both in terms of artistic form and investment. My relationships with special dealers are in many ways reminiscent of my relationships with artisans. I am brought into a world of beautiful things, I am educated, and I am moved to take something home with me.

In the Element of Water

Summer

Water is all motion and depth. It is the most mysterious element, shrouded in an end-less rhythm of solitude. It is vast, covering two-thirds of our planet, and yet it is as complete when isolated in miniature—a bead of dew, a raindrop. Water shows us the translucent colors of tranquillity and the deep shadow of ferocious strength and weight. It is our life source: tactile, flowing, nourishing.

Indonesia

In Bali the fluid, interdisciplinary way of life, where music, theater, costume, food, and architecture all become part of one great art form, is expressive of the embracing flow of the sea. The artisans of Bali are legendary. Most crafts here remain centered around an unending devotion to the honoring of the gods; the decoration of and offerings to native temples have inspired unparalleled mastery of materials ranging from silk to silver.

The Balinese see art and craft as one. Material beauty belongs to everyone in the community. There remains a strong family connection to the diverse map of crafts the island produces: There are lineages of silversmiths in Celuk, palm leaf basketmakers and batik masters in Ubud. Every district has its own signature Ikat-woven patterns for sarongs and its own distinctive style of costume. There is a long tradition of carved and painted wood used to adorn the entryways of homes and temples. The mixture of all these materials into one compelling whole creates a layered aesthetic effect, with wave upon serene wave of visual stimulation. We learn from this how to create a union of materials in our own homes. Every surface will sparkle with magnified texture, as if underwater, as we catch the refracted beauty of our interior landscapes.

A BALINESE SILVERSMITH AT WORK IN HIS ARTISAN STUDIO.

Bringing It All Back Home

In the end, it is the collected experiences of life that matter most and that we seek to bring back home. The objects we acquire, the vignettes we build over years of searching, and the interior style we develop for our homes are ultimately the tools we use to nourish our souls. We create a safe haven in which to store our own histories. Here, at the end of this journey, I center myself in this physical place, and I realize how much that old country phrase rings true, "Home is where the heart is."

I will always take time to praise the materials I bring into my space, to honor the artisans who made them into functional objects, to thank my family and friends for their lively presence, and to pay great respect to the natural world from which my shelter grew. Home will not quite yet be home, however, until I get there myself: I must always return from my travels, turn the key in the front door lock, unpack the treasures I've found, and tell new stories to those who have been waiting for me.

It is my hope for all who have shared this book that you will do the same, every year, through all the seasons, and with the end of each day. Home is your gift to yourself. Take care of your joy there, and leave it for others, as a lasting, most beautiful heirloom.

RESOURCE GUIDE

At Zona, I have had the opportunity to work with a fascinating range of artisans and small craft workshops the world over. Undoubtedly, there are always those outstanding examples who raise the standard of craft itself, whose artistry and workmanship express unusual talent and dedication. Over time I've found that those resources which have become truly classic can translate even the simplest object into something remark-able. Craft of this caliber translates into heirloom spirit for our homes. Here is Zona's guide to many of the finest craft resources we've uncovered, an honor role of sorts with a special mention of what has brought each artisan recognition. In addition, we encourage you to contact us for more information about any resource whom you may be interested in retaining for special projects, or for assistance in liasing with artisans abroad.

ARTISANS

CLAY
Barbara Eigen
150 Bay Street
Jersey City, NJ 07302
TERRA-COTTA PITCHERS

Judy Glaser
112-20 72nd Drive
Forest Hills, NY 11375
ASH KILN CERAMICS

Frances Palmer
313 Georgetown Road
Weston, CT 06883
PAINTED SERVING PLATTERS

Tom Phinney
50 Lincoln Street
Oberlin, OH 44074
PAINTED CANISTER SETS

Sara and Tom Post
604 Barbera Place
Davix, CA 95616
PAINTED SERVING BOWLS

Christine Salusti
430 Greenwich Street
New York, NY 10013
GOLD RIMMED SPIRIT BOWLS

FIBER
Fern Devlin
1323 Dorchester Road
Brooklyn, NY 11226
CHENILLE SCARVES AND THROWS

Michèlle Ratté
RFD 561
P.O. Box 862
West Tisbury, MA 02575
VELVET SCARVES AND HOME FABRICS

Rosemary Watson
17218 Barnwood
Houston, TX 77090
PILLOWS AND SAMPLERS

FOOD
Cafe Beaujolais Bakery
P.O. Box 730
Mendocino, CA 95460
HOT CHOCOLATE

Kathleen's Bake Shop
43 North Sea Road
Southampton, NY 11968
COOKIES

Katz and Co.
6770 Washington St.
Yountville, CA 94599
PRESERVES AND HONEY

Villa Gigli
P.O. Box 307
145 Hot Springs Road
Markleeville, CA 96120
OLIVE OIL

GLASS
Ed Branson
S.R. 189 Hill Road
Ashfield, MA 01330
CRINKLED GLASS TUMBLERS

Ann Morhauser
P.O. Box 8445
Santa Cruz, CA 95061
ANTIQUED GOLD
GLASSWARE

LIGHTING
Liz Galbraith
307A North Third Street
Philadelphia, PA 19106
HANDPAINTED AND HANDMADE PAPER
LAMP SHADES

Richard Hoosin
1121 West Belmont Ave.
Chicago, IL 60657
SHELL LAMPS SHADES

METAL
Kara Varian Baker
2030 Livingston Street
Oakland, CA 94606
SILVER LOCKETS AND SPOONS

Glen Gilmore
P.O. Box 57
Pine Log Rd.
Brasstown, NC 28902
IRON HOOKS

Leigh Morrell
P.O. Box 2114
Marlboro Rd.
W. Brattleboro, VT 05301
FIREPLACE TOOL SETS

Gloria Natale
640 West End Avenue
New York, NY 10024
PRECIOUS GEMS AND METALS

Elmer Roush
Route 1, Box 79-A
Brasstown, NC 28902
IRON NAILS

Phyllis Woods
267 South Stone
Studio F
Tucson, AZ 85701
PRECIOUS METALS

STONE
Chris Curtis
P.O. Box 250
Stowe, VT 05672
FOUNTAINS AND VASES

Stone Forest
P.O. Box 2840
Santa Fe, NM 87504
LANTERNS AND FOUNTAINS

WOOD
Dian Needham
178 Suffolk Street
New York, NY 10002
FURNITURE AND CABINETRY

Peggy Potter
Mad Ellen Road
Waitsfield, VT 05673
SALAD BOWLS

Robert Sonday
P.O. Box 18
Free Union, VA 22940
ROCKING CHAIRS

Taos Furniture Co.
P.O. Box 5555
Santa Fe, NM 87502
PONDEROSA PINE FURNITURE

Edward Wohl
6154 Brotherhood Lane
Ridgeway, WI 53582
BIRDSEYE MAPLE BREADBOARDS

INTERNATIONAL
Carlo Carretti
Italy
FURNITURE AND
RESTORATION

Ceccarelli Studio
Italy
CERAMIC TABLES

Franco Ceccherelli
Italy
ANTIQUE GOLD TRAYS

Magda Guaitamacchi
Italy
CERAMIC FRUIT

Alfred Handel
Switzerland
COLORED CANDLES

John Hardy
Bali
SILVER HOME ACCESSORIES

Renato Guarino
Italy
LEATHER ACCESSORIES

RESOURCE GUIDE

Here's a special listing of some resources who have generously shared their one-of-a-kind collections and knowledge with Zona. Country and antique fairs are great places for adding to or beginning collections, so I've also identi- fied a number of my favorite shows across the country. Get to know your small- er local fairs and flea markets as well; the thrill of the "find" adds immeasurably to the story of a collectible when it comes home with you.

COLLECTIBLES

American Craftsmen Antiques
380A Hubbard Hill Rd.
Gilboa, NY 12076
FINE AMERICAN FOLK ART AND
PAINTED FURNITURE

Josh Baer
116 1/2 Palace Ave.
Santa Fe, NM 89501
ANTIQUE NATIVE AMERICAN TEXTILES
AND POTTERY

Chinalai Tribal Antiques
52 Woodville Rd.
P.O. Box 815
Shoreham, NY 11786
SOUTHEAST ASIAN TEXTILES,
BASKETS, SILVER, WOOD, AND
FURNITURE

Kowalski Clockworks
2225 Triton Lane
Berkeley, CA 94080
WALL AND TABLE CLOCKS HAND
MADE OF FOUND OBJECTS

Bonnie & David Montgomery
R.D. 1 Box 78-A
Jefferson, NY 12093
ECLECTIC AMERICAN FOLK
ANTIQUES

Moose America
97 Main St. Box 7
Rangeley, ME 04970
SNOWSHOES, CREEL BASKETS, AND
OTHER RUSTIC SPORTING ANTIQUES

Nusantara
43 Strongs Avenue
Southeast Asian and Indian
Rutland, VT 05701
TEXTILES, BASKETS, AND SILVER

Parrett/Lich Inc.
2164 Cancl Lane
Georgetown, TX 47122
VINTAGE HICKORY AND
ADIRONDACK FURNITURE

Penny Toys
P.O. Box 226
Winthrop, MA 02152
VINTAGE 1940s CERAMICS AND
KITCHEN APPLIANCES

Pine Tree Hill Antiques
123A Higley Hill Rd.
Wilmington, VT 05363
ECLECTIC AMERICAN FOLK ANTIQUES
AND ARCHITECTURAL ELEMENTS

Morgan Rank
4 Newtown Lane
East Hampton, NY 11937
FINE AMERICAN FOLK PAINTING

Robin Rice
325 West 11th St.
New York, NY 10014
COLLECTED FINE ART PHOTOGRAPHY

Nancy Settel
1304 Arundel Dr.
Wilmington, DE 19808
HANDMADE OLD-STYLE CANDLES
AND FOLK ANTIQUES

Shandor Imports
Route 1 Box 642
Anthony, NM 88021
VINTAGE SOUTHWESTERN PAINTED
FURNITURE

Robert Skinner
P.O. Box 1660
SOUTHAMPTON, NY 11969
ANTIQUE TOOLS

Linda Stein
Lahaska Antique Courte
Rte 202 Box 11
Lahaska, PA 18931
ECLECTIC AMERICAN FOLK ANTIQUES

Three Friends Antiques
152 Tecumseh Lane
Akron, OH 44321
VINTAGE CATCHERS MASKS, RUSTIC
FURNITURE AND SPORTING ANTIQUES

Sue Zippel
Country Corner
6204 Gideon St.
Bowie, MD 20720
ANTIQUE DOMINOES, CRICKET BALLS,
AND OTHER ENGLISH GAMES

COUNTRY ANTIQUE SHOWS

**Cowboy, Ethnographic, and
Indian Markets**
(consecutive shows)
Santa Fe, New Mexico
Don Bennett's Whitehawk, Inc.,
Promoter
805.652.1960

Heart of Country Antiques Show
Nashville, Tennessee
Richard E. Kramer & Associates,
Promoter
314.862.1091

Atlantique City Spring Fair
Atlantic City, New Jersey
Norman Schaut, Promoter
609.926.1800

Round Top Antiques Fair
Round Top, Texas
Emma Lee Turney, Promoter
713.493.5501

May's Antique Market
Brimfield, Massachusetts
Richard D. May, Manager
413.245.9451

J&J Promotions
Brimfield, Massachusetts
Jake Mathiew, Promoter
413.245.9271

Ann Arbor Antiques Market
Ann Arbor, Michigan
Margaret Brusher, Manager
313.662.9453

Rhinebeck Antiques Fair
Rhinebeck, New York
Bill Walter Shows, Inc., Promoter
914.758.6186

Heartland
Richmond, Indiana
Jennifer Smith, Promoter
513.456.5087

Farmington Antiques Weekend
Farmington, Connecticut
Bob & Abby McInnis, Managers
508.839.9735

Riverside Antiques Show
Manchester, New Hampshire
Apple Hill Promotions
603.669.2911

**Adirondack Museum
Antiques Show**
Blue Mountain Lake, New York
Oliver and Gannon Associates,
Inc., Promoter
518.861.5062

American Folk Art Show
New York, New York
Sanford L. Smith and Associates,
Promoter
212.777.5218

York Tailgate Antique Show
York, Pennsylvania
Barry Cohen, Manager
703.914.1268

**Wilton Historical Society
Antiques Show**
Wilton, Connecticut
Marilyn Gould, Manager
203.762.7257

Simply Country
Redmond, Washington
Cathy Hind, Manager
206.821.2526

California Country
Los Altos, California
Bea Teer, Manager
415.948.3642

The Big Fork Antique Show
Big Fork, Montana
Pat Lamb, Manager
406.982.3570

Building a storehouse of ideas for the home always includes seeking out other sensibilities and design philosophies. One of the best ways to confirm a design inclination or expand your core aesthetic is to keep in touch with what's going on in the greater marketplace. I've included here a selection of some of my favorite shops, galleries, and institutes to encourage the process of doing this "visual research." Keep a list of spots like these–places which inspire your eye and spirit–in your own home notebook, and designate them as key destinations to visit, even if they're in your own home town.

SHOPS

Kate's Paperie
561 Broadway
New York, NY 10012
212.941.9816
FINE HAND-MADE PAPER

Throckmorton Fine Art
153 East 61st Street
4th Floor
New York, NY 10021
212.223.1059
VINTAGE MEXICAN PHOTOGRAPHY
AND FINE PRE-COLUMBIAN ARTIFACTS

Selleto's
244 Newbury Street
Boston, MA 02116
617.424.0656
ECLECTIC LIFESTYLE FURNISHINGS

Material Possessions
954 Green Bay Road
Winnetka, IL 60611
708.446.8840
HAND-CRAFTED FURNISHINGS AND
ART OBJECTS FOR THE HOME

Details at Home
1031 Lincoln Road
Miami Beach, FL 33139
305.531.1325
ACCESSORIES FOR THE HOME

Gardens
1818 W35th Street
Austin, TX 78703
512.451.5490
ANTIQUES AND ACCESSORIES FOR
THE GARDEN

American Country
620 Cerillos Road
Sante Fe, NM 87501
505.984.0955
HAND-BUILT FURNITURE AND
LIFESTYLE GIFTS

Cookworks
322 Guadalupe Street
Santa Fe, NM 87501
505.988.7676
FINE TABLETOP AND COOKING
ACCESSORIES

Nonesuch Gallery/Gloria List
749 Alto Street
Santa Fe, NM 87501
505.988.4002
DEVOTIONAL AND DECORATIVE
ARTIFACTS FROM LATIN AMERICA
AND EUROPE

The Hand and the Spirit Gallery
4222 North Marshall Way
Scottsdale, AZ 85251
602.949.1262
CONTEMPORARY AMERICAN CRAFTS

American Feng Shui Institute
108 North Ynez Avenue #202
Monterey Park, CA 91754
213.930.0786
CLASSICAL TRAINING FOR TRADITIONAL
FENG-SHUI

Bell'Occhio
8 Brady Street
San Francisco, CA 94103
415.864.4048
VINTAGE RIBBONS, WRAPPINGS,
AND SPIRIT GIFTS

Bountiful
1335 Abbot Kinney Blvd
Venice, CA 90291
310.450.3620
RUSTIC FURNITURE AND VINTAGE
ARCHITECTURAL FRAGMENTS

Filamento
2185 Filmore Street
San Francisco, CA 94103
415.931.2224
UNIQUE GIFTS AND HAND CRAFTED
HOME ACCESSORIES

Smith & Hawken
117 East Strawberry Drive
Mill Valley, CA 94941
415.383.4415
GARDEN TOOLS, FURNITURE,
AND LIFESTYLE ACCESSORIES

The Gardener
2127 Fourth Street
Berkeley, CA 94710
510.548.4545
HOME ACCESSORIES, GIFTS, AND
FURNITURE

Japonesque
824 Montgomery Street
San Francisco, CA 94133
415.391.8860
MINIMALIST JAPANESE CRAFTS AND
HOME FURNISHINGS

Tail of the Yak
2632 Ashby Avenue
Berkeley, CA 94705
510.841.9891
MYSTICAL AND SPIRITUAL
HAND-MADE GIFTS

Urbino
521 NW 23rd Street
Portland, OR 97210
503.220.0053
TABLETOP ACCESSORIES AND
LIFESTYLE GIFTS

Tenzing-Momo
93 Pike Street
Seattle, WA 98101
206.623.9837
TRADITIONAL HERBAL APOTHECARY

A ZONA LIBRARY

Books are always an important resource for the home. I've put together here a compendium of my favorites, from beautiful coffee-table examples to wonderful children's fables to formative philosophies. Some of the books included represent milestones in the development of my way of thinking about design; others are tried-and-true titles that have become classics at Zona. All are enjoyable both to look at and to read, and all of my own copies are well thumbed through, truly used as resources over and over again. Add these and other titles to your own library, and build an eclectic mix of book styles on your own shelves at home.

American Country: A Style And Source Book; Mary E. Emmerling
Art of Worldly Wisdom, The: A Pocket Oracle; Baltasar Gracian, translated by Christopher Maurer
Barn: The Art of a Working Building; Elric Endersby
The Bed; Alecia Beldegreen
Being Home: A Book of Meditations; Gunilla Norris
The Book of Bamboo; David Farrelly
Cadogan Travel Guides
Caring for Your Collections: Preserving & Protecting Your Art and Other Collectibles; National Committee to Save America's Cultural Collections Staff
Color: Natural Palettes for Painted Rooms; Donald Kaufman & Taffy Dahl
The Contrary Farmer; Gene Logsdon
The Country Woodworker: How to Make Rustic Furniture, Utensils, and Decorations; Jack Hill & James Merrell
Earth to Spirit: In Search of Natural Achitecture; David Pearson

Ethnic Interiors; Dinah Hall
Evolution of Useful Things; Henry Petroski
Feng Shui: The Chinese Art of Placement; Sarah Rossbach
Flowers Rediscovered; Tom Prichard of Madderlake
From the Good Earth: A Celebration of Growing Food Around the World; Michale Ableman
The Glass Pantry: Preserving Seasonal Flavors; Georganne Brennan & Katherine Kleinman
Greens Cookbook: Extraordinary Vegetarian Cuisine from the Celebrated Restaurant; Edward E. Brown & Deborah Madison
How Buildings Learn: What Happens After They're Built; Stewart Brand
Language of the Robe: American Indian Trade Blankets; Robert Kapoun & Charles J. Lohrmann
The Man Who Planted Trees; Jean Giono
A Natural History of the Senses; Diane Ackerman

Off to Sea; Richard Stine
Phenomenon of Man; Pierre Teilhard de Chardin
The Reinvention Of Work: A New Vision of Livelihood for Our Time;
Matthew Fox
Rustic Taditions; Ralph Kylloe
Sante Fe Style; Christine Mather and Sharon Woods
Sara Midda's South of France: A Sketch Book; Sara Midda
Simple Wisdom: Shaker Sayings, Poems, and Songs; Kathleen Mahoney
Simplify Your Life: One Hundred Ways to Slow Down and Enjoy the Things
That Really Matter; Elaine St. James

The Slant Book; Peter Newell
Small Is Beautiful: Economics as if People Mattered; E.F. Schumacher
Stay Up Late; David Byrne and Maira Kalman
Tales of the City Series: Chronicles Abroad; edited by John and Kristin Miller
This House Is Made of Mud; Ken Buchanan
Tibetan Book of Living and Dying; Rinpoche Sogyal
Treasures of the Italian Table; Burton Anderson
A Valley in Italy; Lisa St. Aubin de Teran
Where the Heart Is: A Celebration of Home; edited by Julienne Bennett and
Mimi Lieberman

CREDITS

PHOTOGRAPHERS

WE WISH TO ESPECIALLY RECOGNIZE THE WORK OF THE FOLLOWING PHOTOGRAPHERS, WHOSE IMAGES ILLUSTRATE OUR IDEAS AND INSPIRE OUR IMAGINATIONS:

LIZZIE HIMMEL 15, 17, 18, 19, 20, 21, 27B, 30, 40TBL, 41R, 49T, 54R, 55, 57, 58, 59, 74CTR, 87, 115, 118R, 120, 123, 134TRB, 139, 141R, 143, 144-145, 147, 156, 176, 193R, 202-203 **MARK LANGLOIS** 14, 19, 26, 33, 36-37, 40TR, 42L, 43, 53T, 54L, 63, 114, 122, 134TL, 138, 148T, 154, 161, 163, 164TL **WILLIAM WALDRON** front jacket, 19, 27T, 41L, 44, 49B, 118L, 119, 121R, 124-125, 136, 137, 140, 141L, 142, 148B, 149, 150R, 157T **MARIA ROBLEDO** 2, 5, 6, 32, 45, 64, 67, 73, 78, 92, 93, 94, 95, 96, 97, 99-103, 104, 168, 180, 181, 190, 191R, 198 **TAYA ALLISON** 10-11, 16R, 56, 68BR, 132, 133, 186, 187, 188-189, 190, 191L, 192-193, 194-195 **KATHRYN MILLAN** 6, 28-29, 40BR, 60, 65, 69, 74, 75, 76-77, 86, 89, 98, 113, 126, 130B, 162, 164RB, 167, 178, 179, 204, 208, back jacket **ROBIN RICE** 1, 47, 50-51, 116-117, 121L, 127, 160, 183B **KATHRYN SZOKA** 4, 42, 53B, 61, 68TCB, 85, 105, 128-129, 130T, 131, 133BL, 150L, 169, 196-197, 199 **J. B. GRANT** Nonstock 25, 158 **CHUCK CHOI** 22, 35 **MARTI SAGAR** 16L, 165 **ARLENE SANDLER** 184 **ANDREAS BLECKMANN** Nonstock 24BL **ANTOINETTE JONGEN** FPG International 34 **DENNIS JUNOR** Superstock 48 **ALAN BRIERE** Superstock 62 **JULIE MARR** Nonstock 81 **LESLEY SHIFF** Nonstock 82T **TONE VAZQUEZ** Nonstock 82B **DAVID MIDDLETON** Superstock 90-91 **WALT SENG** Nonstock 151 **LINDA MONTOYA** 107 **LUCA ZAMPEDRI** Nonstock 108-109 **ANN RHONEY** Nonstock 157B **JEAN KOGLER** FPG International 170 **DAVID BURNETT** 171 **ALBERT CALJU** Superstock 172-173 **MICHELE BURCHI** 182, 183T **HARRY GIGLIO** Nonstock 21L **ALINARI** Art Resource 185 J.Hardy Studio 200, 201

We wish to thank the following for their aesthetics:

Victoria Hagen, John Saladino, Vincent Wolf, Martha Baker, Beryl Brown, Robert Dash, Dagne Duval, Zoran, Tony Barreta, Barbara Orbach, Hudson House, Lee Mendel, Diana Epstein, and Millicent Safro

PERMISSIONS

Permission to excerpt material from the following works is gratefully acknowledged:

Appreciations and Criticisms of the Works of Charles Dickens by Gilbert Keith Chesterton.
Copyright © by A. P. Watt, Limited.
Reprinted by permission of Georges Borchardt, Inc., in conjunction with A. P. Watt, Limited

Bamboo by Robert Austin, Dana Levy, and Koichiro Ueda.
Copyright © 1970 by Weatherhill, Inc.

"Danse Russe" by William Carlos Williams, from *Collected Poems: 1909–1939, Volume I.*
Copyright © 1938 by New Directions Publishing Corporation. Reprinted by permission of New Directions Publishing Corporation.

"Final Solioquy of the Interior Paramour" from *Collected Poems* by Wallace Stevens.
Copyright © 1951 by Wallace Stevens. Reprinted by permission of Alfred A. Knopf, Inc.

Home Economics by Wendell Berry.
Copyright © 1987 by Farrar, Straus & Giroux, Inc.

A Natural History of the Senses by Diane Ackerman.
Copyright © 1990 by Diane Ackerman. Reprinted by permission of Random House, Inc.

The Poetics of Space by Gaston Bachelard.
Copyright © 1964 by Beacon Press.

Simplify Your Life: 100 Ways to Slow Down and Enjoy the Things That Really Matter by Elaine St. James.
Copyright © 1994 by Elaine St. James. Reprinted by permission of Hyperion.

Acknowledgments

THIS BOOK WAS INSPIRED BY A VISION OF HOME. FROM THE BEGINNING IT WAS A COLLABORATION BETWEEN A CREATIVE TEAM AND AN EXTENSIVE NETWORK OF RESOURCES.

The birth of this book must be largely credited to our agent and friend Katherine Cowles, who guided and cared so much for us from start to finish. Many thanks to Joseph Montebello, our editor, for his patience and trust; to Eric Baker, for his encouragement and commitment from the beginning, and to Greg Simpson, for a tireless effort at making a beautiful puzzle fit. Special thanks must be given to Lisa Light, who in addition to her writing and editing contributions, was optimistic throughout, and was dedicated to keep the principles of the book in clear focus. I especially want to thank my sister Marti Sagar, who in addition to her direction of photography, kept the team moving and managed to get us all the way home.

Thanks to Maria Robledo for working with us even though she was eight months pregnant. Grateful thanks to Anthony Allison for getting us up early in Texas, and to Taya Allison for her friendship and photographs. Special recognition goes to photographers Lizzie Himmel, Kathryn Millan, and Robin Rice. Additional thanks to Angela Trinkar for her styling contributions and to Jerry Tavin and Janou Pakter for their invaluable photographic stock.

To my close friends and associates, James Mansour, Andrew Ellis, Osamu Anzai, Massimo Rafanelli, thank you for all that you have done. Thanks to the Social Ventures Network, and the Soho Partnership for keeping us feeling responsible. Thank you to my teachers, Paolo Soleri, Buckminster Fuller, Gregory Bateson, Stewart Brand, and Paul Hawken for your inspiration, and Swami Chidvilasananda for her love and wisdom.

In addition, I'd like to acknowledge the Zona management and staff, who remain committed to keeping our stores beautiful and in balance. In particular, thanks to Carrie Van Hise and Lauren Gropp for promotion and editorial assistance. I offer my deepest appreciation to an incredibly dedicated customer base which keeps inspiring us to grow and evolve.

Most affectionately, thank you to my best friend and soulmate, Carolyn Bender, for her daily encouragement to write it down, and for watching over me. Special love to my daughter Sophie for her spirit and grace.

Visit our website. http://www.zonahome.com